DEMETRIOS CAPETANAKIS

DEMETRIOS CAPETANAKIS

DEMETRIOS CAPETANAKIS

A GREEK POET IN ENGLAND

Edited by
JOHN LEHMANN

Biography Index Reprint Series

BOOKS FOR LIBRARIES PRESS
FREEPORT, NEW YORK

PR6005
A4865A65
1971

INTERNATIONAL STANDARD BOOK NUMBER:
0-8369-8055-7

LIBRARY OF CONGRESS CATALOG CARD NUMBER:
73-148208

PRINTED IN THE UNITED STATES OF AMERICA

DEMETRIOS CAPETANAKIS

Demetrios Capetanakis was born in Smyrna on January 22, 1912. He graduated in political science and economics at Athens University and later became a Doctor of Philosophy at Heidelberg University. In Greece he published several philosophic studies, notable among which were *The Struggle of the Solitary Soul* and *The Mythology of Beauty*, before he came to England with the aid of the British Council in 1939. He died of an incurable disease in Westminster Hospital on March 9, 1944.

The photograph which forms the frontispiece
of this volume was taken by Hans Wild.

CONTENTS

INTRODUCTION

By John Lehmann

It is sometimes said, or lightly assumed, that poets and artists who die young, die at their appointed time, and that even if a prefiguring of their death is not to be found in their work, it clearly reveals that they had given the world all they had to give. There are, indeed, poets of whom it seems strangely true, and Shelley is one of them; but there are others, and Keats is one of them, of whom one can admit it only with the greatest difficulty. Their death appears wantonly to cut off a branch at the moment when it promised its most fruitful ripening. If Demetrios Capetanakis had lived, even if only for one or two more years, he would have been able to complete a cycle of work, already planned, which revealed itself more remarkable and beautiful with every advance he made.

He was only too conscious of this himself. It is true that, about eighteen months before his death, he had been passing through a crisis of despair, of agony of spirit for his own happiness and for the suffering of his country, and of doubt of his powers as an artist, which brought him to a point where he did not wish to live any longer. But what is remarkable is that, from that point, in spite of a severe attack of the illness that was eventually to kill him, he turned sharply back into a world of confidence and hope. He was happy, he said it again and again, and even when, in the winter before his death, he was once more too ill to get up, he contrasted his feeling of inner contentment then with the black mood in which the previous attack had found him. He was at work on his poems as long as his strength allowed him, even when it made him giddy and sent up his temperature to correct a single line; he still talked of the articles he intended to write, and for which he had taken elaborate notes; and when in the last few weeks he began to realize, more clearly than his friends who put the thought from them, that he might not recover, his constant preoccupation was with what he had not had time to do, what he still longed to contribute to the life of his time, perhaps even more in other ways, in action and personal teaching, than in literature.

9

He dreamed of writing a novel about London in wartime; he was eager to collaborate in a play, and a book about Shakespeare; those plans were for the future, but already, it seemed, within reach was a book of literary and philosophical criticism. The name he had thought of for it was *The Shores of Darkness*, a name which in itself, if one remembers the sonnet of Keats from which it is taken, implies hope. It was to consist of ten essays, with an introduction and conclusion. He had already written and published the essays on Rimbaud, Stefan George, Dostoevsky, and the Notes on Contemporary Writers, though he thought of enlarging some of them, particularly the last. He had also written the essay on English Poetry in its first form, and had allowed me to publish it in *Penguin New Writing*, though he never saw anything beyond the galley proofs; and the essay on Greek Poetry had been delivered as a lecture, and, though unrevised, can be taken as substantially complete in the form in which it now appears in these pages, including the wonderfully beautiful translations. Of the four other essays, the first two were to be on Plato and Kierkegaard. He had thought for a very long time about these, and had indeed collected a small library of texts and reference books for the work. From the way he spoke about them, to me and other friends, it is clear that he intended them to be as important as those he had already written, perhaps even more important. He was naturally modest about his work, but he was convinced that he had an original contribution to make to the understanding of Plato, and that no interpretation of Kierkegaard yet published in this country had reached the heart of his mystery. To my great sorrow, when I went through his papers after his death, I could find nothing of these two projected essays except the voluminous quotations he had copied out from the original works and the commentaries on them he had found most significant. Everything was ready, but nothing was written. The loss to the world is, I am certain, no small one.* Nor does anything survive of the essay on Friendship, which would have been one of his most eloquent if it contained anything of the enthusiasm and subtle learning he displayed when the theme was under discussion, or of The New World Quest, which was to

---

* At a later date I found some fragments of earlier studies of these two philosophers, very closely argued and characteristic, but unfortunately in no shape for publication.

have been devoted to the literature of the Americas in its most general aspects, and in particular to the novels of Thomas Wolfe in the United States and the critical writings of Eduardo Mallea in the Argentine. For these, there are not even notes to be found; only his carefully scored copies of the books show that they had already begun to take shape in his mind.

There were other articles and lectures among his papers, which weré not intended for the book, but are of very great interest. Perhaps the most interesting is a lecture in French on Proust, a shorter version of an original study of considerable length, in which he analyses the way in which Proust, in the course of his book, continually alters his view about the individual, his anxiety about what can be grasped as real in life the only constant. This I translated, and it was published in *Daylight* (1945) and re-appears in the present volume. There is also a chapter of his un-finished study of Thomas Gray, concerned with Gray's relation-ship with Horace Walpole, and several lectures which he de-livered officially as spokesman of Greece, and which brought him the applause of widely differing audiences, and—what he espe-cially prized in his last illness—an invitation to lecture after the war at London University. If he had lived, I am certain he would also have written about the Spanish mystics, one of his favourite subjects, about many other aspects of French literature, and about Dickens. When he was unable to read anything else, even in his own language, he could still read Dickens; *Our Mutual Friend* was, I think, the last book he read before his death, and he found it, in his own phrase, "a most wonderful book."

Demetrios Capetanakis was a being of the rarest integrity in thought and feeling, and he was incapable of writing anything for the sake of "making literature." His integrity was even per-haps the cause of what may be thought to be a weakness in his work, a certain repetitiveness in argument and an excessive bare-ness of statement. These faults, if faults they are, arose from the strength of his passion to define, to grasp the inmost truth of his subject, whether an experience of his own, or the symbols, intel-lectual and imaginative, of another's experience. That passion was always with him; and the two forms of experience were always closely, indeed inextricably, associated with one another. The peculiar fascination of his studies of poets and philosophers lay in a combination of immense erudition and an unflagging curiosity about life, so that what he wrote out of his erudition had the excitement of something he might have lived through himself. In a sense he *had* lived through it, for being so passionately alive and sensitive in spirit, he had had overwhelming experiences of joy and terror, from which he had drawn certain conclusions about the nature of existence. His previous reading had helped him towards these conclusions; and once he had had the experience he looked back into his reading for corroboration; the tension of the resulting essay came from the thrill of discovering that the key seemed to fit, that sure enough the thread was leading him through the maze. To hold on to that thread was no easy task. He took immense· care in the preparation of each essay, testing each fact as he fitted it into its argument, trying new words to capture something that had escaped the previous words; the effort was exhausting almost beyond the endurance of his frail physique. I do not believe that without astonishing courage and will-power he could have achieved so much during the months when his incurable illness, as we now know, had never really left him.

He intended to call his book *The Shores of Darkness*, because the conviction that grew ever stronger in him was that until one has become aware of the illimitable unknown that surrounds our lives, one cannot understand or properly value existence on earth. He judged artists and thinkers by the extent to which they revealed this awareness in their work. If they had never found themselves on the edge of an abyss where—

> Things which are not are destined to confound
> The Things that are, the fortunes we have earned—

then he did not believe we could learn much from them. Some authors, he would maintain, showed that no experience had ever come to them which caused them to question the nature of reality; others, whom he condemned above all, spent their lives concealing what had terrified them and turned their work into an elaborate unfertile pretence; but he believed that all that was significant in the European mind came from what he called philosophical anxiety. This thesis was already clearly stated in his first published study in English, on Rimbaud, in which the concluding words are: "Nothingness might save or destroy those who face it, but those who ignore it are condemned to unreality. They cannot pretend to a real life, which if it is full of real risks, is also full of real promises." As he went on, he began to formulate a view of English poetry, which he had intimately studied long before he came to Cambridge to write about Thomas Gray. It first appears in the essay on Stefan George. Seeing in George one of the chief spiritual corrupters of German youth, because his mind "was too much of one piece to understand the dialectic mystery of existence, whose reality is born of nothingness, whose light comes from darkness, whose greatest hope is brought about by utmost despair," he set out to define the fundamental error of "state" poetry. In doing so he discovered that the greatest English poetry, though it was like George's poetry in the desire to make existence more solid, and unlike the poetry of such authors as Rilke which seems to dissolve the contours of experience, was fertile where George's was sterile because the desire came from a continual awareness of the limits of the known; because the English poets realized that, as he wrote in his essay on Dostoevsky, "the more questionable everything appears, the more unquestionable the truth of something in man's existence, revealed by suffering and the awareness of nothingness, becomes." This was the idea that he developed in his essay on English Poetry. It was, as he so often emphasized to me during his last illness, rather a series of introductory aphorisms than a connected study, which he intended to complete in the future. He was finding new things to interest and excite him in the English poets to the very end—I remember his enthusiasm about some passages of Blake, and Dryden's translation of Vergil of which he was reading an early eighteenth-century copy in bed—and anyone who heard him talk about his discoveries can only have the deepest regret for what he was unable to get down on paper. Above all one must regret the absence of a fuller study of Shakespeare: he gave only a hint of what he might have written in his few paragraphs on *Troilus and Cressida*.

It was not only our serious poetry that aroused his wonder and delight. "Although it sounds paradoxical," he once wrote, "it is true that comic verse is more apt than serious poetry to make us aware of the tragic side of our lives." He applied to Lewis Carroll and Edward Lear the same test as he had applied to Donne and

Keats, and his friends in Cambridge remember how he used to
quote:

> There was an old man who said "Well!
> Will nobody answer this bell?
>   I have pulled day and night
>   Till my hair has grown white,
> But nobody answers the bell."

He dwelt on this limerick with intense enjoyment, but in the
middle of his laughter would explain that it was really a profound metaphysical statement, and that the old man represented
every poet or philosopher in his search for the truth about life.
His gaiety and sense of humour do not appear very clearly in his
published writings, though his fragment of a novel about Cambridge (written in Greek) is full of witty observation; but one
could not be with him for long without discovering them. I can
remember that when I was about to meet him for the first time,
impressed by the reports of awed undergraduates that he had
read *A la Recherche du Temps Perdu* through fourteen times, I
expected someone of severe countenance and learned manner; it
was an agreeable surprise to find a person entirely unassuming,
full of fun, and ready to throw himself into any literary project
that was on foot, if his friends appealed to him, with unreserved
enthusiasm. He combined with this capacity for enthusiasm an
extraordinary perceptive power, so that one found that what one
wanted or what one needed was continually being anticipated
before one had completely formulated it oneself, and one's inten-
tions were always judged at their highest. It was this quality that
made him the most stimulating of collaborators; it would be impossible for me to attempt to count how often I have profited
from his sympathy and judgment. It was also the genius he had
for giving himself which made him so successful as a teacher of
younger people. One of the happiest periods in his life was when
he went up to the Midlands to help prepare a Friends Ambu-
lance Unit for relief work in Greece as soon as it was liberated.
He made a deep impression on the young men, who learnt to
read, speak and write Greek extremely quickly under his
guidance. That work of his is living now, and will bear fruit for
many years after his country has regained the freedom he so
passionately longed to see.

There must have been moments when he felt very lonely, cut

off from his country and family and knowing only that the most terrible things were a daily event under the German occupation; but he scarcely ever spoke of it, preferring to take part in the lives, the hopes and anxieties of his English friends. For England, after his violent revulsion from Germany and the German philosophy, which for a time deeply influenced him during his studies at Heidelberg, he acquired a devotion and understanding that steadily increased, though he toyed for a time with the idea of going to America; and he even thought of settling here for a long period after the war. If there was no other evidence of his love for our country and civilization, his poems in English would be more than enough in themselves. No one who did not feel assimilated to our life in a supreme sympathy would have been capable of producing them. To me they are one of the most astonishing literary achievements I have ever come across. He was not always sure of certain words and phrases, and used to come to his English friends for advice, say, about the exact difference in shade of meaning between two epithets; his vocabulary was not large, though he was constantly enlarging it, but in spite of this he seems to give the effect of ease and assured control of rhythm and idiom that are probably the most difficult secrets of all to conquer in a foreign language, even if one is already a poet.

His first serious attempt at writing English poetry was "Detective Story," which appeared in *Penguin New Writing*. When he found it was a success he immediately began to plan more and, except during the times when illness prevented him, produced a slow but steady output. He was at work on several poems when he was taken to hospital, but destroyed nearly all these fragments; of the long poem on London there survive only one or two half-lines which were found scattered among his notebooks, and a little more of another long poem on History. The first draft of one stanza of the latter gives an idea of what has been lost:

> No room in history is large enough
> To hold man's greatness. Even the most spacious
> Church is too small for all the hankering
> After eternity and love . . .

And on another page, after many crossings-out and rewritings, a clear—though by no means necessarily final—version of another stanza:

Open the doors which History has shut
And let the winds of uncreative passion
Moaning outside the palace and the hut
Blow in and break the walls of law and fashion . . .

"Detective Story" has nearly all the qualities for which his poetry is remarkable: the direct and natural way in which he *spoke* in the four-line five-beat stanza, the intense dramatic, almost melodramatic situation conveyed so vividly and economically, and always behind it the metaphysical problem suggested with mystery and beauty. People were astonished by it, and disturbed; and that was exactly the effect he wanted to create. Poetry, he believed, must be disturbing before anything else, and because most people do not very much like being disturbed, or made to "feel funny" in the phrase of Gertrude Stein he was fond of quoting, he did not find it at all surprising that true poetry is so often decried or ignored when it is first published. He was contemptuous of work that had only a surface charm, and saw through any involved pretence of being subtle or profound; but if poetry startled by some sharp new vision in which he could find a deeper symbolism, or betrayed philosophical anxiety, then he was ready to forgive even serious technical weaknesses. I think it would be true to say that he never read a poem unless he had read *through* it first. He was always on the look-out for the meaning behind the poem, however concealed the expression and however unconscious the author himself might be of what he was really expressing. It was the same with music, of which he was very fond; one evening at a performance of Tchaikowsky's *Swan Lake* he exclaimed, with characteristic abandon, that Act II was the most haunting thing he had ever heard, because of the questioning of life, a questioning that is never answered, which he found in the music.

His own poems were fashioned directly out of his experience, but it would be a mistake to attempt to read them too literally in that sense. He had such a strong instinct for the dramatic, that there is in nearly every poem that might be read as autobiography a deliberate fusion of the imagined with the real. What was important for him was to make of them "cryptic messages" "with hints of what to hope and how to live," and under their surface simplicity the messages are often not at all easy to decipher. The difficulty is increased because, with his great knowledge of

European thought, it came naturally to him to introduce references, in phrase or image, to the ideas of Plato, or San Juan de la Cruz, or Kierkegaard, or another philosopher. Always, the thought and suffering of Europe was with him, in that perspective of three thousand years since his own nation had laid the first foundations of our civilization, and in them he saw a dominant conception of human life emerging from experiences repeated again and again under changing forms. It was this that gave such force to his interpretation of individual writers, that made him see many of our own writers, such as Thomas Gray or Dickens, in a quite unexpected and revealing light, and that showed up so much of what passes for criticism today in England as shallow and parochial by comparison. He did not reject the chief interpretative instrument of our time, psycho-analysis—he was too much entertained by its results—but he felt that, in his own words, "psychology can explain things, but it never reveals their meaning."

When it became clear to him that he might never finish the long poems on which he had embarked, he abandoned them and summoned up all his remaining strength to write the two pieces which must be considered his testament, "The Isles of Greece" and "Lazarus." He had spoken more than once about his desire to write a poem presenting a truth about Greece which Byron had missed in his famous poem; and now, into those twenty short lines he concentrated all that he felt about his country and her eternally renewed destiny of suffering, lines which are among the most tragic and haunting he ever wrote, and which express Greece perhaps more completely than anything that has been written in our time. This poem we discussed together several times before his death, and the version which has been published received his final approval. The other, "Lazarus," which I find more mysterious and more disturbing than all his other poems, even the supremely beautiful "Abel," he did not want published. He felt that it was full of ambiguities and could have been much improved if he had had time to work on it. Nevertheless I am certain that if he had lived I could have persuaded him to reverse his decision, and after some heart-searching I decided that those lines, formed from the deepest spiritual experiences of his last years of life, should belong to the world.

There was a handful of other poems among his papers, most

of which he had read over to me before he went to hospital, and which I therefore feel no hesitation in adding here to the rest. There are passages of startling beauty in "Guilt," "Angel," "Experienced by Two Stones," "American Games," "Friendship's Tree," and "A Song for Bores," but I think it is important to remember, in reading them, that he might have made changes if he had had a chance to revise them for publication.

The book which has been finally assembled here contains all that he wrote in English during his stay in our country, wherever the state of the manuscripts seemed to me to justify publication. I have excluded his lecture on Greek Art, partly because he was not able to complete it as he would have wished, but chiefly because it was intended as a spoken commentary to a large number of illustrations of Greek painters' works which, for obvious reasons, it would be irrelevant to include; instead, I have put in a translation of an article on the modern Greek painter Ghika, which, though it was written before he came to England, is extremely characteristic and seems to me to contain in essence all that he wished to say about painting. I have also added a translation of a study of Charlotte Brontë, which he published in a Greek paper while he was over here. I feel not only that it falls properly within the scope of this volume, but also that it is of considerable interest as an example of that lighter mood crossing his more serious preoccupations which appeared so rarely after his illness began to gain on him.

In conclusion, I must thank the Editors of *The Listener* and *Time and Tide* for permission to reprint certain poems which originally appeared in their pages, Miss Edith Sitwell, Mr. William Plomer and M. Panayotis Canellopoulos for allowing me to reprint their articles, Professor John Mavrogordato for the extract from his translation of Cavifis' poem quoted in the article on Charlotte Brontë, and Miss Barbara Cooper for her detailed and deeply sympathetic assistance through all the stages of the book's compilation.

PART I

DETECTIVE STORY

THE stranger left the house in the small hours;
A neighbour heard his steps between two dreams;
The body was discovered strewn with flowers;
Their evenings were too passionate, it seems.

They used to be together quite a lot;
The friend was dressed in black, distinguished looking
The porter said; his wife had always thought
They were so nice and interested in cooking.

And this was true perhaps. The other night
They made a soup that was a great success;
They drank some lager too and all was right,
The talk, the kisses and at last the chess.

"It was great fun!" they said; yet their true love
Throbbed in their breasts like pus that must be freed.
The porter found the weapon and the glove,
But only our despair can find the creed.

CAMBRIDGE BAR MEDITATION

WE shall not tell you where the well is hidden.
Cambridge is gay, but unseen courts atone.
The centre of the town is soil forbidden,
Allotted to the don who walks alone.

His rooms in college have a lovely view
And at his parties youth and sherry glitter;
But all he has to say is "How are you?"—
The kernel of the mind is bitter, bitter.

The well of peace disturbs the peace of mind.
The friends are gone to London, yet our hearts
Stayed back to watch the pool of death, behind
Glasses of beer that mirror flying darts.

A SAINT IN PICCADILLY

AMONG the many ways of liberation
The most effective ones are mad or silly.
I met no saint in holy congregation,
But found a martyr haunting Piccadilly.

The world is loathsome to his boundless yearning;
To pierce the heavens is his deadly task;
But prayer is useless when the flesh is burning,
And meditation fails him after dusk.

The call of darkness then assails the room;
The windows tremble and his throat is dry;
A silent trumpet sounds the day of doom,
And all mankind's despair becomes one cry:

"O look at us! how nothingness has preyed
Upon our faces full of cracks and holes
Opening to the void that will invade,
Even the core of our deserted souls!"

The meaning of the cryptogram is faint,
But his desire is clear. He rushes out
And, hungry for the humblest end, the saint
Picks up the lowest person seen about.

THE LAND OF FEAR

BEFORE we leave this deadly Land of Fear
For countries guarded by police, where houses
Are houses, you are you, and here is here,
We must make sure we take with us what rouses
All these suspicions of a weighty nod
Lurking in everything and everywhere.
Because our lives would be condemned if God
Made us a present of His lips, His hair,
And we could not suspect it, but we spent
A night of love with pure eternity,
Thinking that all embraces have an end
When in the morning comes the tray with tea.

PROPHETS

The prophets wept, forgetting all their bliss:

"The days of hope have only led to this.
The pattern of man's dream is mere convention;
We thought the Lover bound to take a Kiss,
That God should look divine in His Ascension.

But God does not conform. The night grows deep
While common sense extols the joys of rest.
We had our human dignity to keep
And sent our souls on this unheard-of quest,

In which there are no dreams and no escape
In holidays from fate, no time to cure
The watchful wound: the precipices gape
And all the answers break or sound impure.

But those who see His face in all its terror
Will die for that, yet not before they give
A cryptic message to the world in error
With hints of what to hope and how to live."

ABEL

My brother Cain, the wounded, liked to sit
Brushing my shoulder, by the staring water
Of life, or death, in cinemas half-lit
By scenes of peace that always turned to slaughter.

He liked to talk to me. His eager voice
Whispered the puzzle of his bleeding thirst,
Or prayed me not to make my final choice,
Unless we had a chat about it first.

And then he chose the final pain for me.
I do not blame his nature: he's my brother;
Nor what you call the times: our love was free,
Would be the same at any time; but rather

The ageless ambiguity of things
Which makes our life mean death, our love be hate.
My blood that streams across the bedroom sings:
"I am my brother opening the gate!"

EMILY DICKINSON

I STAND like a deserted church
That would much rather be
A garden with a hopping bird,
Or with a humming bee.

I did not want eternity,
I only begged for time:
In the trim head of chastity
The bells of madness chime.

Their song blows up a monstrous bee
With burning eyes and beard.
If bees don't look as big as God,
They look at least as weird.

My nights are haunted circuses
Where deadly freaks perform
The trick of stabbed eternity,
The triumph of the worm.

While in the fertile fields of love
Industrious farmers plod,
My days are brooding on man's doom,
The meaning of the rod.

But thought is vain. Man cannot find
What stupid monsters mean.
One night of wrath I closed my door
On God, and called Him mean.

And so I lost Him for a bee;
He lost me for a freak.
Ah, in the grip of boundlessness
The joints of reason creak.

I stand as boundless as a church
That has no door for God,
While in the fruitful fields of love
Ignorant farmers plod.

RETURN

THE traveller returned with empty eyes.
"That is not you!" wept the forsaken friend.
"You promised me the fire that never dies,
And what you bring can only be the end."

The absentee looked at his empty hands
And said: "I give you things you cannot see;
The treasures of the land beyond all lands,
The secrets spied in seas beyond all sea.

Our souls have limits, and our love is bound
To strand where all begins. The silent border
Is strewn with wrecks. My soul was sent·back drowned
Because its dream defied the human order.

You see me here, but I have not returned.
Things which are not are destined to confound
The things which are, the fortunes we have earned.
When all is lost, the Infinite is found."

A SONG FOR BORES

"MIND the steps" was written on the door;
Somebody forgot the kind advice,
Broke his neck, and now he's such a bore:
Gave up all his friends to live with mice.

"Mind the steps" was smiling from your brow,
But our fate is dark and I fell in:
Every time I speak I hear a crow
Summoning all ghosts and all their kin.

"Mind the steps" is written on my door,
But there are no steps and people wonder
Why should one who walks a level floor
Warn of deadly falls and fret and ponder.

GUILT

LISTENER, can you hear the silence howl
And crawl, an endless serpent, round the world?
I see your need for signs and symbols prowl
Along the folded tombs and the unfurled
Bliss of the sky. Hunter and source of light,
Beloved, who did not find the meaning of
The body struggling in its deathward flight
To grasp your groping hand that shook it off,
What does your craving for atonement call
Out of the depths of man-begetting dread?
A phantom, or the thought that after all
Murder means less than nothing to the dead?

EXPERIENCED BY TWO STONES

BLOND smell of sleeping noon and quenched desire;
Stillness of clotted sun and limbs that float
In hairy sweetness, auburn like the fire
Which licked the lips and glided down the throat,
Leaving a lump of bliss stuck in the root
Of coming songs . . .
                    Experienced by two stones
Grown in the core of love's transparent fruit
Round which the burning bee, the summer, drones.

FRIENDSHIP'S TREE

WE met at noon under the Sun's crude stare
Which makes the wrong look equal to the right.
Our limbs were dazzled, and to flee the glare
We bathed our love in blood, our souls in night.

Partners in crime and brothers in despair
We shook the door of death trembling with spite,
But no one opened, and there was nowhere
We could take refuge from excessive light.

We had no other outlet but to wrangle
Over the bloodstained fragments of a thought
Grasped in the depths of dangers dearly bought,

Until at last we found the strength to strangle
The knowledge creeping in our friendship's tree,
And grew in one another blind and free.

AMERICAN GAMES

WHEN I speak of man's dark doom,
Bill from Cincinatti drawls:
"If one makes oneself at home
On this earth, one never fails.

If one wants to play a game,
One must first accept the rules.
If you want to live your time,
You have got to stand the walls

Which imprison us and kill
Those who strike to pull them down.
If you think my wisdom dull,

You have never tried base-ball,
Which has taught me lots of sane
Things."

       I play my life with Bill.

ANGEL

An angel comes bringing a smile as token
Of love, eternal love that fears no danger,
But when we need him most, he says in broken
Language "I cannot help, I am a stranger,"

And vanishes. Angels are not of this
But of another world that knows no pity.
Nothing disturbs their everlasting bliss,
And while man dies they sing their alien ditty:

"We come from nowhere, and our love, as deep
As darkness in our native land, is free
Of human meaning. Man can never reap
Our kisses planted in eternity.

We go nowhere, and those who blindly follow
Our steps are led to nothing. O you fool!
Our sphere of happiness is closed, but hollow,
While broken rings of human love are full."

THE ISLES OF GREECE

THE sun is not in love with us,
Nor the corrosive sea;
Yet both will burn our dried-up flesh
In deep intimacy

With stubborn tongues of briny death
And heavy snakes of fire,
Which writhe and hiss and crack the Greek
Myth of the singing lyre.

The dusty fig-tree cries for help,
Two peasants kill one snake,
While in our rocky heart the gods
Of marble hush and break.

After long ages all our love
Became a barren fever,
Which makes us glow in martyrdom
More beautiful than ever.

Yet when the burning horses force
Apollo to dismount
And rest with us at last, he says
That beauty does not count.

LAZARUS

THIS knock means death. I heard it once before
As I was struggling to remember one,
Just one thing, crying in my fever for
Help, help. Then the door opened, yet no Son

Came in to whisper what I had to know.
Only my sisters wetted me with tears,
But tears are barren symbols. Love is slow,
And when she comes she neither speaks nor hears:

She only kisses and revives the dead
Perhaps in vain. Because what is the use
Of miracles unheard-of, since instead
Of trying to remember the great News

Revealed to me alone by Death and Love,
I struggled to forget them and become
Like everybody else? I longed to move
As if I never had been overcome

By mysteries which made my sisters shiver
As they prepared the supper for our Friend.
He came and we received Him as the Giver,
But did not ask Him when our joy would end.

And now I hear the knock I heard before,
And strive to make up for the holy time,
But I cannot remember, and the door
Creaks letting in my unambiguous crime.

THE POETRY OF DEMETRIOS CAPETANAKIS

By Edith Sitwell

DEMETRIOS CAPETANAKIS died on March 9, 1944, aged just thirty-two years.

With the tragic death of this young being, who seemed even less than his years, and whose mind and spirit were equally beautiful, illuminated, and illuminating, England lost as considerable a writer as did Greece.

It cannot be doubted what that loss must mean to us. Capetanakis was a being destined to be eternally young; his mind, for all its sad wisdom, was ardent, and he had the heroic Greek spirit, with something athletic about it, for he was never in a state of flaccid ease. He was, as a thinker, equally a deep diver and a deep delver. But unlike those beings whom he resembled otherwise so strongly, he did not remain a thing apart from the element he explored. He *was* the element itself.

His gifts as a poet and as a critic seem, to the present writer, equally great. They were of a strange profundity. "Poetry," he said, in the lecture on modern Greek poetry which appears in this volume, "means language—the inmost essence of language." He used English as Conrad, alone among men not born to it, used it —with a native distinction, with subtlety, and a complete understanding of all the shades and inflections of meaning. His muscular system was attuned to it, and in his poems in English the muscles are under complete control, and are capable of any strength and of any delicacy.

He used quatrains with a tight-packed ten-syllable line, or eight-syllable line, as a norm, and with various rhyme patterns; and he produced, in what would seem to be narrow limits, considerable variation. Sometimes he would use a shut-open, shut-open rhyme scheme, and this, in a quatrain with eight-syllable lines, or ten-syllable lines, in which plain words of ordinary speech figure, is exceedingly difficult to handle with success. Dryden wrote of the ten-syllable line: "He" (the poet) "creeps along with ten little words in every line, and helps out his numbers with 'For to' and 'unto' and all the pretty expletives he can find; till he drags them to the end of another line; while the sense is left tired halfway behind it."

This young poet, however, moved with perfect ease within these limits: they seemed to him natural, the body of his poetry.

In "Abel" he used a ten-syllable line, rhymed A—B, A—B. In "Emily Dickinson" he moved most skilfully in quatrains with lines of the eight-syllable, six-syllable norm—the pattern used with much ugliness by Emily Dickinson herself (she was singularly deficient in technique), and by A. E. Housman, whose technique was only very slightly better than hers. With Housman, his form seemed superimposed, a dress rather than a body, something worn as a support for his debility. Emily Dickinson used this form, I imagine, partly because she was deceived by its apparent easiness, partly because the blurring numbing noise of hymns was always in her ears.

One remembers with a start, when studying these two writers, that (as I have said elsewhere) the vast imagination of Marvell's great poem "To his Coy Mistress," and of Mr. Eliot's great poem "Whispers of Immortality," is preserved within the prim eight-syllable line, and this, indeed, even heightens the effect, shows us, in its narrow grave, the eternal skeleton. Wherein lies the difference? In the fact that we feel a controlled and terrible passion underlying Marvell's and Eliot's verses, an explosive force heaving beneath the surface of the line.

Demetrios Capetanakis, in "Emily Dickinson," used quatrains of the eight-six, eight-six pattern, because this was his subject's mode of expression, because he invariably entered his subject's bodily habitation, and became a part of the soul. In this poem he achieved his object in a manner that is almost terrifying.

I shall return to this poem later. At the moment I am concerned with general principles.

In all his poems, Capetanakis used simple words. Sometimes, a colloquialism found its way into the verse: this is the only sign he gives us that he was not writing in his native language, for these exceedingly rare intrusions were there in order to give an impression of ease. It was totally unnecessary.

At the beginning of his essay "A View of English Poetry" he quoted this sentence from Kierkegaard: "Let not our words be like flowers which are in the fields today and tomorrow cast into the oven, not like flowers, even though in their magnificence they surpass Solomon's glory."

With that strange sense of permanence, of an existence beyond fleeting things, he deprived his verse of nearly every physical attribute which might be evanescent.

His words, therefore, were simple, his images few. "Images," as Coleridge said, "do not of themselves characterize the poet. They become proofs of original genius only as far as they are modified by a predominant passion; or by associated thoughts or images awakened by that passion; or when they have the effect of reducing multitude to unity, or succession to the instant; or, lastly, when a human and intellectual life is transferred to them from the poet's own spirit."

Capetanakis had an extraordinary gift for reducing multitude to unity.

These poems have nothing extraneous about them—they have no wrappings, no decorations. In them, his vision is like a flash of light exploring an extremely long deep tunnel, so that we feel certain we know what lies at the end.

Sometimes the light is so blinding that at first we believe we are not seeing. But this is wrong, we are seeing everything—far more than we knew existed.

For all their sad wisdom and their great profundity, the poems are young. But they are never concerned with Spring, with the happiness of youth, or with growth. He was passionately interested in the movements of the soul. He did not see, or was not interested in, the growth of the outer world, the phenomena of Nature. The poems are, as a city is, walled in by stone; but above them is the limitless sky.

They are as much the poems of a city as are those of the otherwise completely different Baudelaire.

The poems of Capetanakis are extremely strange, and the realization of their great strangeness grows upon one, instead of diminishing. The concentration of meaning is so amazing that it conveys, now a feeling of a blinding light (as I have said already), now that of a powerful and terrible darkness, a quintessence of force, almost like a physical presence.

If he had lived he would, one feels, have explored still another kind of tragedy of the heart, and he might have written (allowing for the difference in nationality) such poems as Hardy's "A Trampwoman's Tragedy." It is impossible to compare one poet with another, but the concentration, the darkness followed by a

blinding light, to be found in certain of Capetanakis' poems bear
a certain resemblance to those qualities in Hardy.

"Abel" is an extraordinary poem, packed with meaning, and
of a terrifying depth, comprehension, and concentration. It is on
a universal theme, and in it speaks the pity of a great heart.

The poem changes, with nearly every line, from level to level,
and each is equally impressive, equally charged with meaning.
The blood that is shed is the blood of the whole of humanity; but
sometimes all humanity is merged into one suffering being, one
misunderstood and all-understanding Man, sacrificed to the blind
and bleeding thirst whose cause cannot be found and cured. The
bedroom across which the blood flows is the whole earth—or the
scene of an ordinary sordid murder.

In the first line we are told that the slayer, too, has been
wounded, has suffered. What has caused that wound? Some unknown cause, lying buried deep beneath our present civilization?
We know only that he, too, has suffered, is pitiable . . . is one in
nature and in suffering (as we learn from the next verse) with his
victim. The first line pronounced the theme on which the poem
will be built—the theme which will be elaborated into

> I do not blame his nature: he's my brother
> . . . .
> . . . . but rather
> The ageless ambiguity of things.

From the first line, with its universal import, we pass to the
sight of the individual about to be sacrificed—one of the ordinary
men of a city, looking at the appalling problems of life and death
as if they were a side-show—never seeing that he, too, is involved
—never seeing that his most ordinary occupations held within
them the seed of disaster.

But this is not all. That verse, with its depth and packed meaning, goes far beyond an explanation. As one re-reads the poem
the meaning grows. Fresh implications branch out in new directions. In the terrifying line

> Whispered the puzzle of his bleeding thirst

the central problem of humanity is finding words.

The voice that speaks to Abel is sometimes the voice of mankind speaking to the individual who must die that his brother
may live—is sometimes the voice of democracy, the brotherhood

that may fail us through sheer incomprehension. Sometimes it is the voice of the Statesmen of the world, hesitating on the brink of disaster . . . watching the play . . . waiting for the revelation which will solve the puzzle of the "bleeding thirst"—the thirst that is the result of a wound. Surely there must be some explanation and way of healing? The sacrifice will not be necessary? But no explanation comes, and the poem ends with death inflicted on Man by his brother—the death that leads to freedom.

Compared with this intensely strange poem, with its great profundity, leading us to the centre of the earth, the core of the heart, the central impulse from which thoughts and movements spring, many poems written by the stricken young of our time seem but surface poems. The following lines are part of a poem which was found among Capetanakis' papers after his death, and which appears to be a companion of the wonderful "Abel." It was certainly born from the same impulse:

> We met at noon under the Sun's crude stare
> Which makes the wrong look equal to the right.
> Our limbs were dazzled, and to flee the glare
> We bathed our love in blood, our souls in night.

Sometimes the poems have a force and stillness that would resemble stone, excepting that life is instinct in them. Then from that stillness spring a succession of terrible lines:

> What does your craving for atonement call
> Out of the depths of man-begetting dread?
> A phantom, or the thought that after all
> Murder means less than nothing to the dead?

Actually, the poem from which these lines are taken is one of struggle, of a death-grapple, but lines of an equal hopelessness that yet cannot be defeated occur often in the midst of stillness.

The poem "Emily Dickinson," to which I have referred already, shows a genius of comprehension, a full understanding of the tragedy which nailed a naturally rather flimsy being to the edge of an abyss:

> I stand like a deserted church
> That would much rather be
> A garden with a hopping bird
> Or with a humming bee.
>
> I did not want eternity,
> I only begged for time:
> In the trim head of chastity
> The bells of madness chime. . . .

These verses give some idea of the quality of the poem as a whole. This profundity, this comprehensive deep-piercing sight, this sympathy that was not extraneous, for it fused the inner life of the writer with that of his subject, made Capetanakis a great critic. The tortures of Dostoevsky (the pain of darkness from which light must come), the fears, the worm at the root, of Stefan George—these he suffered and comprehended as if he had lived within their life. In his essay on Dostoevsky he wrote: "We are told in the Book of Job that when once God prided himself to Satan on the 'perfection and uprightness' of a man on earth, Satan remarked: 'Hast thou not made an hedge about him, and about his house, and about all that he hath on every side? . . . But put forth thine hand now, and touch all that he hath, and he will curse thee to thy face.'

"There are two kinds of writers: those whose world is protected by a hedge, and whose truths are unambiguous, and those whose world is not protected by anything against the powers of nothingness, and whose truths are bound to be ambiguous, since, for them, there is no line of demarcation between the things which are and the things which are not. Jane Austen is a typical example of the first Dostoevsky of the second group of writers."

Capetanakis belonged to the second category. There is nothing cosy and sweet about his work.

Always, in his criticism, there is an extraordinary power of illumination.

"Balance," he wrote in "A View of English Poetry," "is the secret of the English genius." He adds, however, that "all great English poets disturb the balance inherent in the spirit of their language. Power in poetry begins with anxiety."

This young man of a high and illuminated soul and great gifts, who had so much to lose, who assuredly had a great future, seems the epitome of the youth who wrestled with Death upon an iron threshing-floor. . . . How significant is the place of that combat. . . . He, too, showed this noble courage in the face of death, this profound wisdom which saw beyond the oncoming dark.

What if

> . . . all our love
> Became a barren fever . . .

as he wrote in the last *completed* poem of his life, "The Isles of Greece"?

In this poem, again, he uses the eight-six, eight-six form. But it is a strange, beautiful poem with its harsh yet unresenting grief, its tragic embodiment. In it he tells us that all is vain—our love, and the life and death of the sun. Even our heroic suffering is in vain.

Yet he had the high and noble spirit of a Greek hero. This will not be lost to us.

Of the loss of those poems that will never be written I cannot trust myself to speak.

PART II

THE GREEKS ARE HUMAN BEINGS

I HAVE heard many impressive things about the Parthenon from Greeks and foreigners, but nothing was as painful to me as the words that Constantin Tsatsos, a young professor of philosophy in the University of Athens, used to repeat in his lectures: "We are interested in the Parthenon, not in the workmen who built it. What matters is the work of art, not human beings." His voice was fiery, his gestures prophetic. It sounded overwhelming, but I was revolted. It was so inhuman that it could not be true. I was very young then, but I was feeling in some obscure way that the Parthenon must be so interesting because it speaks of the interesting people who needed it and made it, and because it can still be mirrored in the eyes of people and affect their lives. What matters is human beings and what becomes of them. That is why, although I want to write something about the modern Greek mind, I am anxious to discuss the people rather than their work. Only if one knows the people can one understand their works. And in this country modern Greeks are little known.

We can even say that the more educated an Englishman is the more difficult it is for him to see Greece of today as she really is. He has done classics at school, perhaps also at the university, and Greece means for him a world of unreal perfection, of suggestive sounds, of fascinating verses and beautiful but intangible forms. Virginia Woolf called one of her essays "On not knowing Greek" because she realized that the Greek of the classical studies had little to do with any Greek historical reality. In this essay she described in a charming way what Greece means to the most cultured circles in England: "It is vain and foolish to talk of knowing Greek, since in our ignorance we should be at the bottom of any class of schoolboys, since we do not know how the words sounded, or where precisely we ought to laugh, or how the actors acted. . . . When we read a stanza in a chorus, the end or the opening of a dialogue of Plato's, a fragment of Sappho, when we bruise our minds upon some tremendous metaphor in the *Agamemnon* instead of stripping the branch of its flowers instantly as we do in reading *Lear,* are we not reading wrongly, losing our sharp sight in the haze of associations? reading into Greek poetry not what they have but what we lack? Does not the whole of Greece heap itself behind every line of its literature? They admit us to a vision of the earth unravaged, the sea unpolluted, the maturity, tried but unbroken, of mankind. . . . Back and back we are drawn to steep ourselves in what, perhaps, is only an image of the reality, not the reality itself, a summer's day imagined in the heart of a northern winter."

Such dreams can have a tremendous importance in the forming of a civilization—and among them the dream of Greece has been the most effective—but their interference with everyday life can be sometimes misleading. A Greek in England feels often embarrassed when he is introduced to classical scholars. Their eyes, accustomed to read Greek texts, do not see clearer for that; instead of seeing the Greek who stands before them as he really is, they fold him in so many verses they know by heart, in so many names of heroes, poets, philosophers or artists they admire, in so many memories from their school or college life, that the poor Greek, who feels himself decked with so much that has but little to do with himself, is overwhelmed. It is still worse when he feels that he is not only associated with the classical studies of the other, but is also compared to the ideal of a Greek the other holds. He feels that the proportions of his body are mentally compared to the proportions of a Greek statue representing a god, a hero or an athlete, and that his nose puzzles the other because it is not as straight as the famous "Greek nose." The modern Greek is very proud of his ancestors, of course, but he does not like much to be considered only in relation to them. He is more or less conscious of being the product of a much longer history than the few centuries of ancient Greece—he also is conscious of belonging to his own age. He is a reality here and now, and he may feel uneasy when his questioner tries to place him by transposing him to a world of dream. Imagine a Greek seeing the person to whom he is introduced receiving the formal words: "This is X, from Greece," as if they were the lines by which Marlowe's Faust is introducing the ghost of Helen of Troy to his guests:

Gentlemen,
For that I know your friendship is unfeigned,
You shall behold this peerless dame of Greece,
No other ways for pomp and majesty,
Than when Sir Paris cross'd the seas with her,
And brought the spoils to rich Dardania.

Such scenes are not rare in the circles of the highly educated. But the opposite extreme, perhaps more misleading, is also frequent in them. Some others who do not want to be deceived by their classical associations refuse to associate modern Greece with any of the great periods of her history, and they insist on seeing in her only her less attractive aspect. More than a hundred years ago, at the time of the great enthusiasm for Greece, Maria Edgeworth, the Irish novelist, described this attitude in one of her characters. "Greece is a dangerous field for a political speculator," she made him say; "the imagination produces an illusion . . . ; the reflected images of ancient Grecian glory pass in a rapid succession before the mental eye; and delighted with the captivating forms of greatness and splendour, we forget for a moment that the scene is in reality a naked waste." Mrs. Edgeworth's character was wrong; what was happening in Greece at this time was more fascinating and more significant than anything that the imagination could produce. In the two Greek poets of the time, Solomos and Calvos, one could hardly find any "naked waste." But Mrs. Edgeworth's character preferred not to know anything; it is so much easier and so much more effective to be the man who does not want to be deceived. It is not surprising that today many people have adopted this same attitude towards Greece. By doing so they think they show realistic, sober minds. They forget that this attitude obscures the view as much as enthusiasm, besides being less noble. If they happen to be admirers of T. S. Eliot, for instance, their representation of a modern Greek is the M. Eugenides of the lines:

Under the brown fog of a winter noon
M. Eugenides, the Smyrna merchant
Unshaven, with a pocket full of currants
C.i.f. London: documents at sight,
Asked me in demotic French
To luncheon at the Cannon Street Hotel
Followed by a weekend at the Metropole.

Many business men in London must have met T. S. Eliot's M. Eugenides, the rich vulgar Greek merchant, and they no

4

doubt think of him when they hear of Greece. That is very misleading, as misleading as to think of the age of Pericles when
one hears of Greek history. The Greeks of today are neither lingering specimens of a race that worked wonders two thousand
years ago, nor a Balkan people without any past and without
any roots in the history of their land. If one wants to understand
them, one must connect them to the whole rather than to some
periods of their history, and see them at the same time as
modern Europeans. It would be a great pity if the Greeks were
still what they were at the time of Pericles. The history of their
sensibility would be much too poor.

A history of the Greek sensibility through the ages—analo-
gous to Virginia Woolf's "Orlando," that delightful history of
the English sensibility from the Elizabethan age to our days—
would be an extremely rich and thrilling work. The Greek
Orlando would be among other things a hero of the Homeric
age, divine in his manly strength and weakness; a youth of the
Academy of Plato with a mind burning with love; a soldier conquering Asia and the world of wonders under Alexander the
Great; a fastidious poet in Alexandria handling words as if they
were pearls; the man of taste under the Romans who preferred
the peaceful and limited happiness of life in his own country to
the "crowd" of Rome; a plotting courtier in Constantinople or
a Byzantine monk painting emaciated saints in a background of
gold; a scholar refugee teaching Greek to the Italians of the
Renaissance; a brigand under the Turks, living on the moun-
tains "in the company of the woods and the wild beasts" and
winning his freedom by his sword; a "great interpreter" at the
Sultan's court, a refined European in an oriental country ignoring Europe; a hero of the war of the Greek independence be-
lieving that "one hour's freedom is better than a long life of
slavery"; an enthusiastic democrat of the nineteenth century;
and finally a twentieth-century man full of vitality, who only a
short while ago proved, in the way he fought the invaders of his
country, that "he still has a soul in his breast."*

The Greek through his history has had so many experiences,
so many ups and downs—nothing human, neither the lowest nor
the highest, was refused to him. The only thing that never

* See the poem by P. Prevalakis quoted at the end of *An Introduction
to Modern Greek Poetry.*

changed in Greek civilization was its male character. There were times when the Greek could be called effeminate, as during the Hellenistic and Roman periods, but Greece never lost its manliness. In no time of Greek history do we find women setting the tone—as in the France of Louis XIV, for instance—unless we go back to prehistoric times in Crete. Historians said that it was a feminine civilization—but it is too long ago, no one can know anything certain about it; besides, we are not interested in history whose traces cannot be found in the present.

What matters is not history as history, but human beings. What matters is the Greeks of today and what will become of them. What now matters is humanity and what will become of it.

GHIKA

At the second Pan-Hellenic Art Exhibition, the work which held me in front of it longer than any other—for hours, in fact—was Ghika's "Island Landscape."

The painter, who has long been recognized in Paris, has always seemed until now to belong exclusively to European painting, without having any particular tie with his own particular country, Greece. But with the picture which he is now exhibiting to the Greek public he shows, without ceasing to speak the European language, that he has given it a new depth, using it to express the spirit of the landscape of his own country.

Ghika's symbols no longer have the general abstract character, which they had till now. They are closely linked with the soil and sky of a definite place. But it is just for that reason that their artistic significance has increased. The more precise the language of art becomes the wider becomes its meaning, and the deeper. I am sure that Paris, where Ghika's æsthetic efforts were always followed with such interest when they had no particular geographical connection, will understand just as easily his painting today, which may be called the Metaphysics of Greek Nature. There is no opposition between the Greek and the European. The more we become ourselves the greater our significance to others. In Ghika's latest works we cannot with certainty distinguish the European from the new Greek elements. Ghika's deep European culture gives new Greek forms a meaning which they would not otherwise have; but without the new Greek forms the European culture would perhaps be lost in the abstract and the general. What is certain is that these works contain the realization of a rounded personality which impresses us with the force of its character, its wisdom and its magic. What Christian Zervos wrote in 1933 in *Cahiers d'Art* about this painter, that "nobody can tell yet what the final success of his plans and his efforts will be, how far he will drive along the adventurous path of art, how much he will depart from today's objectives, what the progressive phases of his art will be," no longer holds good today. At this moment Ghika knows exactly what he wants. He is no longer trying to find his way—he has his feet firmly on it—and even if his work still presents itself to us as a perpetual series of experiments, the reason why it does so is precisely that the essence of his art consists in æsthetic and metaphysical experiment. It is this essence that I should like to indicate in the present note.

From the time of Cézanne and Van Gogh painting took on an indisputably metaphysical tendency. The impressionism which these two great painters surpassed was only concerned with the transient and deceptive form of visible things. The impressionists wanted only to capture this form at one fugitive moment and to transfer it with an attractive effect to the surface of a canvas. They only wanted to achieve the magic of a surface, whose significance is that of the visible and the fugitive. But man has a deeper need, the need of what is stable and eternal. If painting were no more than the illumination of the transient it would mean the deadliest despair. From such despair art was saved by Cézanne and Van Gogh. The former struggled to find a technique which would reveal the pictorial essence of things—instead of their visible nature—and the latter tried to show us what the world meant to him. Both efforts were purely metaphysical. Painting no longer tried to show what things look like, but what they are and what they mean. The painter's eye tried to see within and behind the perceptible forms of the universe a meaning far beyond the limits of that universe, in the dark unknown from which we come and towards which we are on our way. This abyss frightened many artists, who saw in it a terrifying Nothing. In their eyes the world is nothing but discord, ugliness and pain. The painting of many German expressionists is a cry of indescribable terror and agony. But other painters saw in this unknown, not Nothing, but an unexplored yet indisputable will which governs and controls the universe and makes it a genuine Cosmos, which properly means Order. One of them, and a very conscious and penetrating one, is Ghika.

He requires his universe to be the creation of a divine will. The conflicts which tear our life apart and which reveal perilous fissures all around us, that threaten us with total destruction, do not have in his eyes the importance which they have for others. Behind them he does not detect a great void in which we are liable to be annihilated: he discerns a higher will which can only aim at order, harmony and continuity. Its laws are not obvious to everyone, but their force cannot be disputed, and it would be worth while devoting our lives to conceive what they are. Ghika at least has devoted himself to this. His painting tries to express the will of God: the deeper order of the universe. His attitude in the midst of life reminds us of Dürer's "Melancholy." Withdrawn into himself in the same way, far from the din of common men, who do not even imagine the existence of anything deeper than what they can see, surrounded by his tools and his instruments, he plunges his gaze into the earth and the sky, in an effort to conceive an order of patterns and a harmony of colours which could express the order and harmony of the universe. But the wonderful thing is that this creative exploration does not take place in the nocturnal twilight of Dürer's etching nor in the violent contrast of light and shade which tears across the visible universe and directs our gaze to the mystery of the unknown, like the laboratory of Rembrandt's "Alchemist"; rather it is carried out in the shadowless expanse of a sun-washed Greek day on the islands. There is no room there for any trickery. No chiaroscuro is used to suggest the magic whose force we feel so profoundly. The miracle is revealed nakedly in the sun, and demands even more light so that none of its form may be concealed. But the more its form is revealed the greater becomes its mystery. In Ghika's "Island Landscape" my eye was attracted by a black hill in the blue background. "That black shows up all the luminosity of the landscape," the painter explained to me. All the luminosity and all the *depth* of the canvas, I thought, the transparence of whose colour draws us on to the unknown where nothing can be other than black. I remember a little black jar in the corner of another canvas. It gave me the impression of cool water in the burning heat of midday—the coolness of death in the fire of life. One ought to stay hours together before every work of Ghika. The longer one's eye rests not only on the general composition and harmony but on every line, every shape, in many cases every tone, the more their magic and their mystery increase. If it were only a matter of optical delusion (doubly delusive since it would have no meaning except as another presentation of the delusive appearance of visible things), then one's interest would quickly be exhausted. But from what I have said so far it is obvious that Ghika's painting abhors all delusion and aims to bring one into immediate contact with the very essence of the spirit. This essence can only consist of the laws by

which the unexplored divine will holds together and controls the
universe, and which the artist must struggle to conceive and to
express by means of his art. In this way, by approaching the
divine spirit, he can purify his own soul, and the soul of any
spectator worthy of the name. That is what Ghika tries to do.
One can easily imagine the strain of the effort. In an article which
he recently published about man's struggle to conceive the laws
which really direct the universe, he made us an unconscious confession about his own personal struggle—he gave us a vivid picture of himself in his loneliest moments of concentration and
creation: "It seems to be impossible for a man to make movement and progress in this life, except by means of curved or
broken lines. Insuperable obstacles preclude him from a straight
line. He is obliged to avoid them, to make and abandon one
attempt after another, to try various ways of overcoming them, to
attack the difficulties methodically or by surprise, to discover the
weak point of every problem, sometimes even to imagine it
already solved in order to solve it, and often to succeed only by
force. That is the way of all technique: the way which every
technique, every science, must necessarily follow: the submission
to matter which is so humiliating, but at the same time so
human" ("The Third Eye," December 7, 1937). With these words
he expresses in the clearest and most moving manner (but without a trace of sentimentality) how much the artist remains a man,
a limited force, even in his most superhuman struggle: the effort
to conquer the divine will. His words show us something else
that is fundamental too: the meaning to this artist of the perceptible forms of the spirit. The straight line, the broken line,
the curve, are symbols to him which illuminate our path with a
light from another universe. We feel this all the more when we
turn our eyes from his words to his drawing. Even his colouring
indicates something similar. His painting struggles to be a
symbol of all that is highest. And in that it differs from surrealism. Surrealism is also a realization of symbols, but their
purpose is to express the depths which are to be found beneath
the individual consciousness. The symbols of Ghika's painting
try, on the contrary, to express the heights which are beyond all
consciousness. Surrealism turns the eye downward; Ghika's painting turns it upward. The former is a pseudo-scientific romanti-
cism which, despite all its longing for escape, remains imprisoned

in human nature, while the latter is the æsthetic metaphysics, whose aim is to pass beyond the limits of the flesh and to enjoy the freedom of the divine—the true science, the highest wisdom. And the wonderful thing about Ghika's work is that his æsthetic and metaphysical efforts never cease to be art. Stand in front of one of his latest works—for instance, the picture on exhibition at the Zappion. It will be a pleasure not only to your brain, which will enjoy it too, but even to your body. You will live through the joy of a brilliant day on the Greek islands—a joy, too, whose significance is not transient, because the permanent order and harmony which create it are themselves nothing transient. One feels the coolness of the island envelop one's body like a breath from another world, a world beyond the furthest limits of our universe, a world which our human abilities can never reach.

RIMBAUD

Alone I watched the exit from the world . . . *

I

POETS, like Rimbaud, who tell us that to cling so much to our everyday happiness and comfort may not be the right way of existence are necessary not only during undisturbed times, but also, and perhaps more so, during times of distress. Because even in our greatest distress we always manage to find shelter in some form of happiness and make ourselves more or less comfortable in it. We know that from the nights of the worst air raids.

One of the most disappointing truths we are taught by this war is that "not even war can frighten us enough," as Auden remarked a little while ago. I confess that I had not expected it to be so. "Well," I thought when the war started, trying to hope for the best, "it will be horrible, but if it will be as horrible as to frighten and wake up the mind, it might become the salvation of many. Many are going to die, but those who will survive will have a real life with the mind awake." And I represented the war to myself like those "Dances of Death" engraved by mediæval artists to frighten and keep the people's minds awake with their *memento mori*. But I was mistaken. It is really a great mistake to believe that what can be effected by a work of art could also be effected by the works of war. The *memento mori* of the war is addressed to the flesh rather than to the mind. I quite realized this during my first night of raid. It was the animal in me that was shivering; it was not the mind shuddering before nothing-ness. And I could not help thinking what a mistake it had been to believe that a bomb could shake the mind. The war is very frightening, but it is not frightening enough. The fear cannot go deep enough to shake the mind. The grief cannot go deep enough to make the mind bleed. It seems that as long as the mind sleeps, no horrible situation can be grasped in all its horror. One might get physically frightened, but this fear is only the fear of the flesh, of the animal, not the fear of the man facing his fate.

The most important moment in Rimbaud's development was

* This line is from a poem by J. R. Ackerley.

53

when he realized, to his horror, that human beings are condemned to live perpetually in a happiness they can never escape.
This discovery horrified him because he also knew that happiness is an obstacle to a real existence; it gives us a feeling of
security and comfort, which allows our minds, so lazy are they, to
retire and sleep undisturbed. But a life with the mind asleep is
not a real life. Rimbaud did all he could to keep his mind awake.
This led him to extremes and the story of his efforts to live a real
life is an extremely tragic and, perhaps, deplorable adventure.
But it is stimulating to recall it once more. Not because Rimbaud's way can be a way for us. He cannot be taken as a pattern.
He was an exception that cannot be followed. How many of us
could have the force—"the force of despair"—to dare what he
dared? Besides, we must not forget the terrifying fact that the
stirring part of Rimbaud's life was his adolescence. He wrote his
first important poem before he was sixteen, and the last line of
his last literary work before he was nineteen. During these three
years of boyhood he went so far in thought, words and despair,
that no human being can ever go further. Such a courage cannot,
and must not, get lost. We need it, because even during this time
of unhappiness we still manage to cling to happiness too much,
and we must have somebody to tell us that this might be the
wrong thing after all.

II

He was not yet sixteen when happiness was revealed to him
in such a way that he not only enjoyed it, but also got hold of it
and expressed it in the eight lines of his first real poem. The
poem was called "Sensation," but the title "Bonheur" would
have been as suitable. The eight lines are a complete symbol of
what we could call the order, the "happiness" of the world:

> Par les soirs bleus d'été j'irai dans les sentiers,
> Picoté par les blés, fouler l'herbe menue :
> Rêveur, j'en sentirai la fraîcheur à mes pieds.
> Je laisserai le vent baigner ma tête nue.
>
> Je ne parlerai pas; je ne penserai rien.
> Mais l'amour infini me montera dans l'âme;
> Et j'irai loin, bien loin, comme un bohémien,
> Par la Nature—heureux comme avec une femme.

The body of a youth in harmony with himself and with the

world, undisturbed by thought which always leads to questions and doubts breaking all peace and all beauty; a youth's beautiful body united unreservedly with nature, is perhaps the most successful symbol of the order of the world, of "happiness." Its perfection, like the completeness of some works of art, makes us forget that there might be something wrong with the world. It makes us forget the dangers, the splits, the illogicalities, the hostility, fight and destruction. It makes everything seem reasonable and secure. It is happiness and a symbol of the harmony of the world.

A dangerous symbol, it seems. Perhaps there is no such harmony. Perhaps if there is, we must not know about it or count on it. Perhaps the symbol is inadequate. Anyhow, Rimbaud, who had the revelation of this symbol in a blue summer evening and believed in it with all the ardour of his youth, had to suffer much for it. The consequences were terrible. Was it perhaps a crime? Was it perhaps an error? he asked later on, when he tried to find out the reasons for all his suffering. But no one can answer such questions. We cannot know if suffering is the consequence of the right or the wrong thing. We cannot even know which is the right and which is the wrong thing. The only thing he was certain about was that the revelation of a symbol of order, harmony and happiness, "beauty," was at the root of all the disorder, the divisions and the suffering he experienced.

"Jadis"—he confessed—"jadis, si je me souviens bien, ma vie était un festin où s'ouvraient tous les cœurs, où tous les vins coulaient.

"Un soir, j'ai assis la Beauté sur mes genoux. Et je l'ai trouvée amère.—Et je l'ai injuriée."

We do not exactly know what made him pass from the "happiness" of his first poem to the despair of the poems which followed it. Whatever it was, it must have happened during the summer of 1870. That was a bad summer for France—a time of threat of war, of war and disaster. What broke Rimbaud's happiness was probably the simple discovery—but we must not forget that he was a boy of fifteen then—the very simple discovery, that this symbol of happiness, the beautiful and undisturbed body of a young man, can be destroyed in a meaningless way by the bullet of a meaningless war. Rimbaud expressed this revelation in another of his poems, in his well-known "Dormeur du Val": A young man seems to be sleeping in a pleasant nook of verdure, sun and coolness. You would say he was in the arms of nature. But he is pale and his mouth is open. The harmony of his body is disturbed and he is not in harmony with nature. He is cold. He has two red holes in his right side.

The symbol of happiness was a deceit after all. There cannot be any real order in a world in which its finest manifestation is destroyed so unreasonably and unjustly. It did not make sense. A belief in the meaning of a beautiful body can no longer be held after that. Its promise was a lie, and the boy, who had believed in it with his whole being, had now to pay for it with the utmost despair.

"Sur toute joie pour l'étrangler, j'ai fait le bond sourd de la bête féroce.

"J'ai appelé les bourreaux pour, en périssant, mordre la crosse de leurs fusils. J'ai appelé les fléaux, pour m'étouffer avec le sable, le sang. Le malheur a été mon dieu. Je me suis allongé dans la boue. Je me suis séché à l'air du crime. Et j'ai joué de bons tours à la folie."

III

The body, that proved so deceitful, was attacked by Rimbaud with a savage fury. The frantic blows against it were blows at his own deadly wound, but that made them the fiercer. There were no limits to his despair. He wanted to tear himself to pieces and he was doing it by tearing the deceitful symbol to pieces. The young man's body with the pure lines and the perfect proportions was now replaced in his poetry by corpses in decomposition, by the outraged bodies of the old and the hungry, by the fat and perspiring bodies of the bourgeois, by the diseased bodies of the prostitutes, by the impure and imperfect bodies of children, by bodies of women in which he saw only the animal. It was for months and months that Rimbaud wrote almost nothing but poems showing the human body in its most shameful and disgusting forms. He showed the bodies of the hanged with a small piece of flesh trembling under their chins, but stripped of their vests of skin—"le reste est peu gênant et se voit sans scandale"—he showed the bodies of "Les Assis," of the very old men, who, defaced by tumours, smallpox, green circles round the eyes, vague patches on the sinciput like the leprous efflorescence on

old walls, have grafted their fantastic frames to the large black
skeletons of their chairs in epileptic embraces:

> Oh, ne les faites pas lever! c'est le naufrage.
> Ils surgissent, grondant comme des chats giflés,
> Ouvrant lentement leurs homoplates, ô rage!
> Tout leur pantalon bouffe à leurs reins boursouflés!—

he showed the bodies of the "poor at the church," of those "soup-
eaters" with a stupid and beggarly faith running out of their
mouths like saliva; he showed the body of a "Venus" getting
out of her bath, with its many disgusting details and the famous
ulcer on the anus; he showed the bodies of the puffy bourgeois
strangled by the heat at the open-air concerts of the municipal
orchestra; he showed the impure body of the small boy who

> vaincu, stupide, il etait entêté
> A se renfermer dans la fraîcheur des latrines:
> Il pensait là tranquile en livrant ses narines,

and the body of the young girl with the sad eyes and the yellow
forehead, who also spent the eve of her first communion in the
lavatory full of desires that soiled her heart and her flesh for
ever. But the dream of the man with the message from a better
world written on his face was too deeply rooted in Rimbaud's
nature to be easily torn out from him. From time to time,
between two fits of rage against all bodies, he dared to dream of
this man he would have liked to meet or he would have liked to
be himself. He invoked the dead for a noble cause, "pale from
the mad kiss of Freedom"; he invoked those "millions of Christs
with the dark and sweet eyes." But in doing this his voice was
broken, regretful, like the voice of one deserted by the beloved.
He saw himself as Ariadne abandoned on an island by Theseus;
he saw himself as Ophelia betrayed by everything:

> Ciel, Amour, Liberté: quel rêve, ô pauvre Folle!
> Tu te fondais à lui comme une neige au feu;
> Tes grandes visions étranglaient ta parole.
> —Et l'Infini terrible effara ton œil bleu.

IV

All this despair, all this suffering, all this destructive passion,
were not in vain. A new revelation was dawning out of all this.
This scourging, this tearing of the human body opened fissures

in it behind which one could guess an unknown, terrifying world. The appearance of beauty had spoken to the boy of a luminous reality underlying all appearances. Now the appearance of ugliness hinted upon a dark reality behind everything. That was the "terrible Infinite" which frightened Ophelia's—Rimbaud's—blue eye. The unknown underlying all appearances. The inconceivable reality perceived through the wrinkles and distortions of the human body. And not only through them. It was not only the human body cracking before the boy's eyes. All possible shelters were splitting, letting him see through the gaps the fascinating horror of the unknown, from which we have come, to which we go, in which lies the meaning of our lives. The shelter of his home could not keep him any more. From August, 1870, to May, 1871, when he became quite conscious of the message he had to give to the world as a poet, he ran away from his home three times, leaving behind a perplexed and desperate mother. The first time he was caught by the police as soon as he arrived in Paris and sent back to his mother; a week later he ran away again towards Belgium; the third time he managed to get to Paris, but he was driven back by the fatigue of a fortnight's tramping in the Parisian streets. This return did not mean that his home could be a refuge to him any longer. Everything was cracking. The fate of his country was a problem during this time. France was covered with bleeding wounds. Yet the fate of Justice, represented by the revolution, was still more problematic. There could be only one refuge for the young poet: the elder friend who with the warmth of his affection and the strength of his greater knowledge could have protected the boy from the horrors of the shelterless. But the friend did not respond. It was Monsieur Izambard, Rimbaud's schoolmaster, who had shown some interest in him as long as he had him as a pupil and afterwards. Rimbaud hoped everything from a more intimate relation with him, and between his second and third flight from home, when he was tortured by the calls of the unknown trying to make him run away again, he sent the most passionate appeal to the elder friend—the appeal of a human being sinking into nothingness and trying for the last time to grasp at something, at the only thing that could save him.

But the disillusionment was cruel. The friend for whom the boy would have liked to die chose for himself a life in comfort.

He wrote to the boy that "on se doit à la Société," and managed to be given a good job. Rimbaud saw through him without being able to find any trace of the aspiration he would have expected from him. What else could he do than answer to his "Cher Monsieur" with a sobbing spite: "Vous revoilà professeur. On se doit à la Société, vous m'avez dit; vous faites parti des corps enseignants; vous roulez dans la bonne ornière.—Moi aussi, je suis le principe: je me fais cyniquement *entretenir*; je déterre d'anciens imbéciles de collège: tout ce que je puis inventer de bête, de sale, de mauvais, en action et en paroles, je le leur livre: on me paie en bocks et en filles . . . . Je me dois à la Société, c'est juste—et j'ai raison. Vous aussi vous avez raison, pour aujourd'hui. . . . Maintenant, je m'encrapule le plus possible. Pourquoi? Je veux être poète, et je travaille à me rendre *voyant*: vous ne comprendrez pas du tout, et je ne saurais presque vous expliquer. Il s'agit d'arriver à l'inconnu. . . ."

V

To give up the world and become a seer of things out of the world—that was the only possible solution.

He had tried once more to find what he wanted—something absolute—in the world, in the absolute friendship with the person he needed; but this person proved incapable of such a relation; such a relation proved impossible; friendship had also split, letting the eye catch a glimpse of the unknown behind it. The orders of the world were full of gaps, pointing to another inconceivable reality lying behind them. One could never find happiness; there is only a realm of pure unhappiness behind everything. Nothingness was sending its mute call from everywhere; it seemed to be the only possible absolute; everything else seemed a delusive appearance, a surface behind which one always found, omnipresent, omnipotent, the same thing: nothingness. The boy was fascinated. His despair had led him to the discovery of what seemed to be the only reality, the realm of absolute despair, of nothingness. When he was a little younger he used to read adventure books about explorers in mysterious countries. Why not try himself to become the explorer, not of a particular unknown country, but of the Unknown in general, of the endless unknown surrounding our world, surrounding our lives, surrounding all our gestures or thoughts, everything we see or touch. Besides, even if this prospect would not have appealed to him, he would have had to become this explorer, because there was no other solution for him. His despair had brought him to the verge where there are only three alternatives, which are no alternatives after all, since all of them come to the same—the alternatives of death, madness and what was called by Rimbaud vision of the unknown. All three mean a leap into nothingness. They are three different forms of the same thing. One could interchange the names without giving a false impression of the facts. Death, madness and the vision of nothingness are three equally dark, inexplicable, incommunicable, experiences transcending the world. To become the explorer of their country is to venture into madness and death. If Rimbaud had to do it, it was not because he wanted a dangerous amusement to give him an exciting time, but because there was no alternative for him; it was thrust upon him by a necessity which terrified him. One never faces nothingness because one likes it—no one can like it —or because one thinks that it is the right thing to do. It suddenly comes and one has to submit. "Les souffrances sont énormes," Rimbaud wrote in this same letter of disappointed friendship we last quoted, "les souffrances sont énormes, mais il faut être fort, être né poète, et je me suis reconnu poète. Ce n'est pas du tout ma faute. Je est un autre. Tant pis pour le bois qui se trouve violon."

"I is somebody else." The great and significant things of our lives—love, creation, death—come to us by reason of something else, not because of our own will; they are an inexplicable necessity, sometimes so illogical that our reason refuses to accept it. Rimbaud watched himself becoming a "seer" of the unknown with terror. It was forced upon him by a despair he did not freely choose. No one wants to be crushed by suffering, but suffering comes whether we want it or not. To be a poet was for Rimbaud to be crushed by suffering, but what could he do since it happened to him. "Tant d'*égoïstes* se proclament auteurs; il en est bien d'autres qui s'attribuent leur progrès intellectuel!" he contemptuously exclaimed in another letter. The only real intellectual progress is given to those who have had a revelation of the unknown, and this revelation cannot be

ascribed to their own powers. It is always thrust upon them by
extreme suffering or by some similar unaccountable experience.
The young poet does not invade the country of poetry because
he wants it; he rather is invaded by the unbearable vision:

> Il sent marcher sur lui d'atroces solitudes.
> Alors, et toujours beau, sans dégoût du cercueil,
> Qu'il croie aux vastes fins, Rêves ou Promenades
> Immenses à travers les nuits de Verité,
> Et t'appelle en son âme et ses membres malades,
> O Mort mystérieuse, ô sœur de charité!

We repeat it, there could be no other solution for him. It was
this—to be a poet, a seer—or madness, or death—and *this* was
also madness and death in some way. But it was a kind of madness that made reason richer than it was before. It was a vision
of nothingness, and only those who have faced nothingness can
also see reality as it really is. Because, those who do not dare to
face nothingness are not really awake, and they cannot see anything with really open eyes. Only the terror before nothingness
can shake us and make us realize what it is all about. Otherwise
our real self sleeps in the remotest corner of our inside, and we
spend our life in a way that is not our own.

That is what Rimbaud realized at the most imporant turning
point of his development.

VI

He realized that all his suffering had not been in vain. He
suddenly felt—was it because he was becoming a "seer"?—that
in the middle of all these sleep-walkers he was the only one
awake. The others, given to their small everyday happiness, were
living without really living; they had not suffered; they had not
the least apprehension of all the dangers by which they were
surrounded; they were walking on the brink of an abyss they
could not see, since they were asleep—since they were happy.
But he was awake. He had suffered and nothingness had been
revealed to him. He could see all the unfathomable darkness of
the day and hear the terrifying threat of the most peaceful
night. He was becoming a seer. He knew things that no one
seemed to apprehend. But he wanted to know more and more of
them. He wanted to become more and more awake until he

5

sank into what he called "la plénitude du grand rêve," until he
was given the complete revelation of the unknown. But for that
he had to be always on his guard not to let his real self fall asleep,
not to surrender himself to the sweetness of everyday life or to
any other happiness. He had to beware of all forms of happiness.
"Le bonheur a été ma fatalité, mon remords, mon ver," he wrote
later on in his confession. Happiness was revealed to him as our
greatest enemy.

> J'ai fait la magique étude
> Du bonheur que personne n'élude,

Rimbaud said of happiness—of the orders of our lives.

> Ah! je n'aurai plus d'envie,
> Il s'est chargé de ma vie.

> Ce charme a pris âme et corps
> Et dispersé les efforts.

> L'heure de la fuite, hélas!
> Sera l'heure du trépas.

And he was right. Only death can deliver us from most of the
orders of our lives—the order of our body, for instance. Only
death can deliver us from our happiness. Human beings are
condemned to spend their lives in happiness, that is in the order
of the world. World, the opposite of chaos, means order, and
order makes us comfortable and secure—that is happy. No one
can conceive us outside the happiness secured to us by the world.
And we cannot escape. Our body, for instance, is one of the
orders of the world. How could we escape from our body? But
this unavoidable happiness is our curse, our "fatalité," as Rimbaud said. It is an evil power which subjects us by flattering the
laziness of our bodies and minds, sends our real self to sleep and
sees that we lead a life that is not our own. We lead the life of the
order of our office, of the order of our meals, of the order of the
social conventions, of the order of our car, of the order of the language we speak, and beyond them of the order of day and night,
of the order of the seasons, and so on and so on—we never do or
live anything that does not belong to this or to that order of the
world which has but little to do with our real self; and it is
pleasant to live so and we enjoy it, and our real self indulges in
its laziness and we neglect the things that really matter. We

forget that we belong to a world of appearances and that nothing-ness lurks behind everything. We forget that side by side with all this happiness of ours there are disorders, injustices and illogi-calities, which ought to make questionable all possibility of a real order in the world. We usually prefer to ignore all this and enjoy our happiness, often calling ourselves "unhappy," because it is in the order of things, and consequently of our happiness, to do it. But Rimbaud was disgusted and worried by all this. He felt that since he saw things clearer than his neighbours his duty was to help them. He felt that he had to keep himself awake, not only for his own sake, but also for the sake of the others. He knew that he had a message of extreme importance to give to the world—a message that could wake up some people. But for that he had to become as awake as possible himself; he had to see things much clearer than he had done up to now; and then he had to express himself to communicate the vision. That is how Rimbaud experienced the moral as well as the psychological necessity to become a "seer," a poet.

This is what, later on, he called his "charity."

VII

The task was to tear up happiness, to have a vision of what is hidden behind it and communicate it to the world. He had to create the poetry of "pure unhappiness"—a poetry fighting the orders of our life, denying them, breaking them, trying to pierce through them into the unknown. "Le poète se fait *voyant*," he wrote, "par un long, immense et raisonné *dérèglement* de *tous les sens*." If the poet wants to speak of real things and not of appearances, he must try to tear up the curtain spread before our eyes by our senses and catch things behind them. That can be tried only by "le long, immense et raisonné dérèglement de tous les sens." The happiness of our everyday vision given to us by the order of our senses must be destroyed to give place to the real vision. The happiness of our everyday experience must be shattered to give place to the real experience. "Toutes les formes d'amour, de souffrance, de folie; il (le poète) cherche lui-même, il épuise en lui tous les poisons, pour n'en garder que les quintessences. Ineffable torture où il a besoin de toute la foi, de toute la force surhumaine, où il devient entre tous le grand malade, le grand criminel, le grand maudit—et le suprême Savant!—Car il arrive à *l'inconnu*! . . . Il arrive a l'inconnu; et quand affolé il finirait par perdre l'intelligence de ses visions, il les a vues! Qu'il crève dans son bondissement par les choses inouïs et innommables: viendront d'autres horribles travailleurs; ils commenceront par les horizons, où l'autre s'est affaisé!"—That was the optimistic dream of the boy: that he could become the explorer of the inexplorable; that even if he would not be able to advance very far in it, others would follow his steps and go further and further until the task, begun by him, would be achieved; as if anything could be achieved in nothingness; as if there was a beginning and an end in nothingness; as if one could leave steps in nothingness; as if the inexplorable was explorable. But he believed in the impossible. He was too young, too full of the enthusiasm of a martyr, and he hoped that he could achieve something that no one had dared to dream of before.

His first experiment in this exploration of the inexplorable was "Bateau Ivre." He was still in his native town when he wrote it. The great adventure had not yet started, but the poem gives a foretaste of it. There are cries of despair in it one cannot forget:

> Mais, vrai, j'ai trop pleuré. Les aubes sont navrantes,
> Toute lune est atroce et tout soleil amer.
> L'âcre amour m'a gonflé de torpeurs énivrantes.
> Oh! que ma quille éclate! Oh! que j'aille à la mer!

There also is an unforgettable cry of promise and hope. Out of all this despair a new, better, stronger life might come:

> Est-ce en ces nuits sans fond que tu dors et t'exiles
> Million d'oiseaux d'or, ô future Vigeur?

The poet was trying to know the unknown, hoping that in its depths one could find secrets that might change mankind. Poetry was the power that could find out and reveal these secrets. The thrill of this hope is obvious in "Bateau Ivre" and gives to the poem a stirring vibration. It was written a few days before the boy left Charleville for Paris, where Verlaine was expecting him, and where he was to begin his terrifying experiments with "pure unhappiness" in poetry and life.

VIII

The "Illuminations" are the experiment with "pure unhappiness" in poetry.—It is true that to the superficial reader
they do not look as "unhappy" as the earlier poems of Rimbaud's
period of scourging and soiling of the human body. They do not
sound like cries, screams, sobs and moans of despair like the
earlier ones. But their unhappiness is much deeper—it is a deliberate, methodical, total unhappiness. The poet's destructive
passion is now directed, not only against the human body, but
against all the orders of the world, against the whole world. The
"Illuminations" are an attempt to blow up all appearances, all
orders, all forms of the world, which make our happiness. They
are an attempt to blow up all happiness and make a work of
pure unhappiness out of the debris and fragments of the ex-
plosion. But how strange! These fragments are not pieces of dirt
and ugliness. They are not disgusting like the pieces of a blown-
up body. They have a strange, fascinating beauty. They are like
precious stones and broken tender whispers. "Cela commença
par quelques dégoûts"—by the poems insulting the body—"et
cela finit par une débandade de parfums"—by the "Illuminations."—"Cela commençait par toute la rustrerie, voici que cela
finit par des anges de flamme et de glace."—"J'avais été damné
par l'arc-en-ciel." It is strange indeed. The "Illuminations," this
work of pure unhappiness, seems full of a fascinating happiness
of its own. This heap of fragments from all possible orders, which
should reveal to us what lies beyond all orders of the world,
beyond all happiness, rises before us like a glorious rainbow
speaking to us of the sweetness of pleasure. All these fragments,
that should look like symbols of the unknown, become, thus
isolated and broken, more glittering and precious, and if they
remind of anything, it is of the luxuries and pleasures of the
world. How they shine, how they sparkle before us, all these
diamonds and this foam, these drops of sweat and these eyes,
these rays and this floating hair, these flames and this herbage
of steel and emerald, these white, burning tears and these ring-
ing, flashing dream flowers, these swarms of gold leaves, these
balls of sapphire and these angels of the "Illuminations"! Real
fireworks to make us happy. And to think that they were meant

to fight our happiness, to make us wake up and grow out of it!
What a failure! Rimbaud knew that he failed in this; he also
knew why.

Que comprendre à ma parole?

we read in one of the versions of his poem on happiness.

Il fait qu'elle fuit et s'envole.

"Il" is "le bonheur." He had tried to fight happiness, but one
cannot fight it. He had tried to do it with language, but all language is order, happiness. Besides, the happy people who read
it do not give much thought to it. Why should they trouble
themselves to go beyond the surface and get disturbed and
frightened and lose their feeling of security, especially if the
surface is so pleasant, so satisfactory by itself?—The "Illuminations" are stirring and frightening to those who know what they
were really meant for, but to most of their readers are only
poetry of a strange beauty. Happiness is always the winner. Even
the works created to destroy happiness become one more happiness in the world. The "Illuminations" missed their aim. The
experiment with pure unhappiness in poetry was a failure.

But Rimbaud was at the same time attempting an experiment
with pure unhappiness in life. Was this a failure too? What did
come out of it?

IX

Much was said about Rimbaud's friendship with Verlaine.
People made a scandal, a case out of it. They discussed the facts,
they tried to explain them psychologically, they condemned or
they defended. But they missed the point. Psychology can explain things, but it never reveals their meaning. And Rimbaud's
friendship with Verlaine is one of the most significant friend-
ships we know. We could call it a "metaphysical friendship."

It was an attempt, on Rimbaud's part, to base a relation
between two human beings, not upon values and conventions of
the world, but upon the unknown reality transcending the
world. This reality is a terrifying darkness, and their friendship
became something extremely dark and terrifying. No one of the
"orders" which make a friendship "happy" can be found in it.
There was no reason, no logic in it. They were attached to one

another and they seemed to hate one another, and they could not part and they could not live together, and they were parting and they were coming together again and they were always trying to destroy one another. And there was love, strong and real—so strong and so real that it went beyond happiness. It seemed to be coming from the darkness that is beyond the world, and it had the frightening depth of the unknown. The eyes of the two friends were always turned towards the unknown. Rimbaud had succeeded in compelling the other into the relation of pure unhappiness he wanted. Poor Verlaine—"poor Lélian!" said Rimbaud—he could not quite understand what it was all about. But there was a necessity in all this and he had to comply. He had to suffer, to live in terror, anxiety and despair, to feel always on the brink of an abyss, but his intuition was telling him that there was a meaning in all this and that his friend had thrust all this upon him because he really cared about him. "À côté de son cher corps endormi," Rimbaud made him say, describing him as the "foolish virgin" in his "Season in Hell," "que d'heures des nuits j'ai veillé, cherchant pourquoi il voulait tant s'évader de la réalité. Jamais homme n'eut pareil vœu. . . . Il a peut-être des secrets pour *changer la vie*? Non, il ne fait qu'en chercher, me repliquais-je. Enfin sa charité est ensorcellée, et j'en suis la prisonnière. Aucune autre âme n'aurait assez de force—force de désespoir!—pour la supporter, pour être protegée et aimée par lui." Although Verlaine could not quite understand his friend—"j'étais sûre de ne jamais entrer son monde," says the "foolish virgin" again—he could see that Rimbaud was torturing him and himself not because of selfishness, cruelty or hatred, but because of love, kindness and "charity." He could apprehend a terrifying secret under all this —a secret that might change life, "the laws and the morals" of the world. But in spite of this partial comprehension, we cannot say that Verlaine was the right, the strong enough, partner for Rimbaud's experiment in applied metaphysics. Verlaine got so exasperated by all this incessant watchfulness, this continual terror, this uninterrupted circling round nothingness, that he could not stand it any longer, and in a moment of dizziness he attempted to kill his friend. He shot him twice. The first shot hit Rimbaud on the wrist, the second entered the floor. This happened in Belgium in July, 1873, a year and six months after

they met for the first time in Paris. Verlaine was arrested and
Rimbaud returned home overwhelmed by the feeling of his
failure. He had believed that he knew secrets to make life
richer, stronger, more real, but they proved to be means of death
only. They had not even the power to unite him with his friend
in an indissoluble way. "Quelle vie! La vrai vie est absente.
Nous ne sommes plus au monde," had cried this friend in his
distress. Because, if the friendship was a failure, what Rimbaud
had aimed to achieve through the relation, to go out of the
world, had been a success. Rimbaud did succeed in going out
of the world. He expected everything from it. But it proved
more disappointing than all else. It was his worst error.

X

To go out of the world was Rimbaud's great desire ever since
he discovered how deceptive life in the world can be. When
through the tearings in the shattered human body he caught the
first glimpse of the unknown beyond the world, he was fascinated. But he was hasty in his conclusions. He thought, since the
world is only a world of appearances and since behind all these
appearances we always find the same dark and inconceivable
something, the unknown, this unknown must be the reality in
which we should live if we wanted to have a real and undeceived life. And determined to conquer this real and undeceived
life he set to work. We already know how. By deranging everything—as much as he could and as many as possible of the orders
of the world. He made himself homeless, an expatriate, an out-
law in love and in poetry, the sworn enemy of reason and happiness, he did everything he could not to belong to the world, to
abstract himself from it, always on the look-out for an opportunity to go completely out of it. Not by suicide. He did not
want to go out of the world as nothing into nothing, but as a
traveller going to an unknown country to explore it, to know
it and to live in it. Poetry and friendship were the two most important ways he tried for this exit from the world. He went both
these ways to their limits, beyond which there is neither poetry
nor friendship, but eternal silence and separation. This border-
line was a terrifying waste: "Les sentiers sont âpres, les monti-
cules se couvrent de genêts. L'air est immobile. Que les oiseaux

et les sources sont loin! Ce ne peut être que la fin du monde, en
avançant." "La terreur venait. Je tombais dans des sommeils de
plusieurs jours, et, levé, je continuais les rêves les plus tristes.
J'étais mûr pour le trépas, et par une route de dangers ma
faiblesse me menait aux confins du monde et de la Cimmérie,
patrie de l'ombre et des tourbillons." He really was "ripe" for
the exit from the world. And this exit was given to him as it
was given to Teresa de Jesús, to Juan de la Cruz, to Meister
Eckhart and to others. But it was felt and described by him, not
as a night of bliss, not as a night of union with God, as it was
described by Juan de la Cruz,

> —oh noche amable más que el alborada,
> oh noche, que juntaste
> Amado con amada,
> amada en el Amado transformada!—

but as a night in hell: "Ah ça! l'horloge de la vie s'est arrêtée
tout à l'heure. Je ne suis plus au monde.—Extase, cauchemar,
sommeil dans un nid de flammes. . . . Decidément, nous sommes
hors du monde. Plus aucun son. Mon tact a disparu. Ah! mon
chateau, ma Saxe, mon bois de saules. Les soirs, les matins, les
nuits, les jours. . . . Suis-je las! . . . Je meurs de lassitude. C'est
le tombeau, je m'en vais aux vers, horreur de l'horreur! Satan,
farceur, tu veux me dissoudre avec tes charmes. Je réclame, je
réclame! un coup de fourche, une goutte de feu. Ah! remonter
à la vie. Jeter les yeux sur nos difformités. Et ce poison, ce baiser
mille fois maudit! Ma faiblesse, la cruauté du monde!" "Ah!
to go up to life again!"—What a failure, the worst of all, to
have sacrificed everything for *this*, and then to find out, when
this was attained at last, that it was nothing, that it was less than
the least of the things one sacrificed for it. And to want to go
back to the world where one had nothing left any more. Rimbaud was not a mystic. It was true that he was longing for the
absolute, and that, like the mystics, he tried to find it by going
out of the world. But when he succeeded at last in going out,
he found no bliss in this, like the mystics. On the contrary, he
could not bear the nothingness he met there. That was no life.
That was no existence with one's real self awake. That was losing
oneself in a realm of all negatives: of darkness, of silence, of
immobility, of sterility—of death. There was nothing to be explored in it: there was no space. There was nothing to be known

in it: there was nothing at all. His hope that all the "mysteries" —"religious or natural, death, birth, future, past, cosmogony, nothingness"—would be unveiled to him was vain. One could not even get frightened by it. It is nothing, and one is nothing in it, and it cannot rouse any feelings in one, and one cannot feel anything about it. That was certainly not what Rimbaud had been looking for. It was the opposite. This sphere of pure unhappiness proved to be as dangerous to a real life as the happiness of the world. And Rimbaud felt ashamed for having deserted the world. He had wanted to save himself, his friend and others from the deadly power of happiness and make them live a better, purer existence. But he had been mistaken in the way he chose for it. "Suis-je trompé?" he had to ask when he saw the results of his efforts. "La charité serait-elle la sœur de la mort pour moi?" Instead of saving his friend, instead of making him really live, he led him to the way of destruction, and he could not even stay by him, to help him at this moment of extreme distress. He had to fail him and move on alone.

But the experience was not without fruits. Rimbaud realized that if there is any truth at all we must look for it in this world, it cannot be in nothingness, and that our duty is to find it and realize it in our everyday life. The hope that after all this "it would be possible for him to possess truth in a soul and a body" was expressed by him in the last lines of his "Season in Hell," the confession of his experiments and their results he wrote as a last contribution to literature before he left France and Europe for a life of a man of action in exotic countries. He had nothing else to say to the world. Since he had dared to reach with his words the limit beyond which there is nothing; since he had bruised himself and shattered his language upon the impenetrable wall of the eternal silence, why should he ever speak again? He knew that no one can ever go beyond what he had said. There are no words, no symbols, no thoughts for this beyond. There is only silence.

XI

I do not dare to ask what is the moral of this story. No one can ever know what our lives mean. Everything is ambiguous. One can say that nothingness is a dangerous thing and that Rimbaud

was justly punished for having meddled so much with it. Somebody else might say that nothingness is the only thing that can
save us, since it is the only thing that reminds us of the meaning of our lives, and that Rimbaud was admirable for the courage with which he faced it. Both these thoughts have a truth in
them. What matters is not the conclusion we draw—in another
moment we might draw the opposite conclusion with equal
truth. What is important is to get really interested in such
things, to dare to think of them, to dare to face the problem of
our existence. Nothingness might save or destroy those who face
it, but those who ignore it are condemned to unreality. They
cannot pretend to a real life, which, if it is full of real risks, is
also full of real promises.

STEFAN GEORGE

Hier sitz' ich und forme Menschen
Nach meinem Bilde . . .
GOETHE: Prometheus.

I

STEFAN GEORGE, the most Germanic perhaps of all German poets, was undoubtedly one of Hitler's forerunners. It is true that he never showed any sign of sympathy with the Nazis. It even seems that he never answered the letter which, as the story goes, Goebbels wrote to him, soon after the Nazis came to power, asking him to become the official poet of the party and the nation. He was then abroad and never returned to his country. No answer of his could have been clearer. Although his country, as we shall see, meant so much to him, he preferred to die abroad rather than return to a Germany so different from his vision. Nevertheless, he was one of those who prepared the way for the Nazis. His poetry is a predominantly fascist poetry, and he was a dictator poet. He considered himself a Führer, and we find in his work almost all the main characteristics of the Nazi régime. One of the main motifs of his poetry was the leader principle—no one has ever taken so much trouble to convince people that the most important and natural human relationship is the relationship between the leader and the follower—and long before the world became familiar with things such as a new myth, a new religion, a new Reich, a new order, the initiated in George's poetry knew all about them.

As a person George was intolerant, inhuman, consumed by the thirst for power. Unfortunately we do not know much about his more personal life. It is said that before he died he destroyed most of the letters he had written to friends, and the ones among those not destroyed which were published since his death do not reveal much of the poet's really intimate life. They are impersonal, formal, reticent—like the portraits we have of him. What these portraits tell us is that his appearance must have been most impressive—"er hatte etwas Imperatorisches in seinem Wesen," one of his friends wrote of him once; he was tall, as a leader should be, and he had the sculptural and powerful face of a lion, which concealed rather than revealed his inner life. It was a mask, the mask of a leader, that was going to help him to make a myth of himself. He was a poseur. Unfortunately the story of his life can be only the story of a lifelong pose. Even his poetry was a pose. Those who read poetry in order to come in contact with a human being will be disappointed with George. We cannot be sure that even in his most human-sounding moments George was not acting, scheming, calculating. Even when we read this line that seems so full of human warmth:

Seitdem ich ganz mich gab hab' ich mich ganz,

we feel that he may have written it because he wanted to make other people give themselves up completely to him.

I never met Stefan George, but I came to know some of his spiritual sons, his disciples, and in them I saw reflected the image of their Master. When I went to Germany, and that was in 1934, the Master was already dead, but one could see some young people very much like one another, as if they were brothers, about Heidelberg. And they were spiritual brothers. They were the spiritual sons of the Master.

I was much struck when I saw one of them for the first time. They were really worth seeing. They would come down Neue Schlossstrasse almost dancing, tall, graceful and athletic, with the head thrown back, as if they were trying to avoid the sight of common humanity, and with their eyes full of a strange and disturbing fire, as if they were the guardians of a joyful secret that was burning their souls. Sometimes they were in S.A. uniform, that was perhaps more becoming to them than the dark, austere, almost clerical suit they usually had on. National socialism had already disturbed the order of the George circle.

It was the time when the inscription over the main entrance of the New Heidelberg University, "Dem lebendigen Geist," was taken away and replaced by a new one: "Dem Deutschen Geist."

I did not know yet what all this meant. I was very young and I was amused and impressed by what I used to call the Nazi madness. It seemed to me a strange, imposing and diverting madness. I did not know yet how dangerous it was. And in the same way I was impressed, amused and intrigued by the George people. I did not know yet what inhumanity was hidden in them. Today I know better about Georgeism, as we all know better about Hitlerism. My personal contact with the George people was one of the most bitter experiences of my life.

II

When George was eighteen he wrote a few naïve, sentimental, childish lines, which could hardly be called a poem, but which contain the fundamental experience of his youth, that was going to make him a poet:

> I wandered through deserted, dismal spaces,
> Letting my life flow meaningless away;
> There was no aspiration in my heart
> And nothing seemed to speak to me of Beauty.
>
> When suddenly I saw—who could have told me—
> A godlike image hovering before me,
> I felt a tremor in my inmost being
> And Cupid planted his victorious flags.

All poets are made poets by an experience we could call revelation, which during their youth has moved them so deeply that they have to try to express it and speak about it to the world. Wordsworth was made a poet by the revelation of nature, Baudelaire by the revelation of sin, Rimbaud by the revelation of happiness and unhappiness, and George by the revelation of the miracle of the human body. What suddenly shook the young boy out of an indifferent, meaningless and dull existence, and made him discover the meaning and magic of life, was the "godlike image" of a body, which woke up his senses, his emotions and his mind. This "godlike image" was not a merely external reality, of course. What moves us most is mainly our own creation—and George was so deeply stirred by his own ideal of a beautiful body, all his life long he was so intensely haunted by it, that he lived only for its sake, he lived only in order to change it into an unquestionable and imperishable reality. Later on he once suggested that it was this ideal which determined the whole rhythm of his existence.

Unfortunately this need to find, to create and possess this ideal as a tangible reality was so strong in him that it led him to

aberrations. In order to become the unquestionable possessor of
the body he was dreaming of, he wanted to become as powerful
as possible. And the personal ambition to dominate, to become
the master over other people, is one of the most destructive
human impulses. No fertile human relationship can be based
upon it. To use political power for personal ambition is a crime.
To use the power of poetry for personal ambition is also a crime
—a crime of the spirit—against which one must be warned.

It is not a coincidence that the Germany which produced
Hitler has also produced George. Political and spiritual fascism
were not an accident in the political and spiritual history of
Germany. They were prepared by a long, strong and persistent
tradition of German thought and vision—a tradition deeply
rooted in the darkest and most animal parts of the German soul,
and to which even those of the Germans who are usually considered as "great," humane and lovers of freedom, belonged.
There are people in this country who think with nostalgia of the
divided, humane, cultured Germany of Goethe's time, when her
only aspirations seemed to be aspirations of the mind, and when
her only achievements seemed to be achievements of thought.
But it was during this time that poetry and metaphysics were
opening the way to what is happening in Germany today. What
else than a dictator of the spirit was Goethe during the last
period of his life? Think of his admiration for Napoleon and of
his intolerance towards the creative powers of a younger generation. One cannot forget how he treated Kleist, as one cannot
forget how inhumanly "humane" Schiller treated Hölderlin.
But what else than a prophet of spiritual fascism was Hölderlin
himself, when he criticized the civilization of his time and asked:

> O, when, when
> at last will the flood open
> over the drought
>
> But where is he?
> to conjure up the living spirit.

This long, desperate, messianic expectation of spiritual Germany that "He," the "One" who would save the nation and mankind, was coming, was one of the forces which prepared the way
for spiritual and political fascism. Cries like Hölderlin's lines we
quoted above—and there are innumerable similar cries in

German literature—gave the right to people like Hitler and George to become political and spiritual dictators.

III

In spite of this long German tradition behind him, George did not find his way to spiritual dictatorship at once. Such a dictatorship was not the poetic fashion of the time, and very young people let themselves be influenced by the tendency of the moment rather than by the strongest urge of the past. What attracted young George, the tall, striking-looking boy with the beautiful hands and the belief that there was a gulf between himself and the common people, during the earlier period of his poetic career, was the *fin de siècle* æstheticism which was at the time the fashion among the artistic circles of Paris and London. George's earlier poems were another version of the æstheticism of the time. But what makes them so interesting is that, although one can easily recognize the French and English models in them, they could never have been written by a French or English poet. They are unmistakably Germanic.

In the imagination of the German boy, weak Des Esseintes, the famous hero of Huysman's novel *À Rebours*, and snobbish Dorian Gray, changed features and became Heliogabalus— Algabal, a tyrannic Emperor of Roman decadence. This Emperor had much in common with Des Esseintes, the æsthetic young man "fuyant a tire d'aile dans le rêve, se refugiant dans l'illusion d'extravagantes fééries, vivant seul, loin de son siècle dans de milieux moins vils"—and Algabal's castle was not much unlike Des Esseintes' house in Fonteney. Yet Algabal had his æsthetic castle built, not because he wanted to flee into a world of undisturbed dream, but because he wanted to be the Master in a world "in which there would be no other will besides his own, in which he would be the master even over the light and the weather." While Des Esseintes and Oscar Wilde liked strange and monstrous flowers, and by doing this they recognized Nature when it became eccentric, Algabal preferred not to have them in his world, because the growing even of the strangest and most monstrous flower would depend on natural laws, and he would have hated to see anyone or anything obeying a law other than his own:

My garden needs neither air nor warmth,
The garden I built for myself,
The frozen swarms of its birds
Have never known the spring.

The trunks are of coal, the branches of coal,
There are gloomy fields within gloomy borders,
The never gathered burden of fruits
Glitter like lava in a pine grove.

In this artificial, suffocating, barren world young George thought for a moment that he could satisfy his boundless will to power. No other power besides his own, not even nature, would be there to prevent him from being the absolute Master—the Creator, the Owner and the Ruler. His ideal of a superior human being, of a being with a princely body, would be realized in himself, by his own body.

But George was not a sterile nature, and this solution that could satisfy only arid minds which, unable to create something in the realm of reality, prefer to flee from it and deceive themselves by dreams in the void, could not satisfy George's boundless need for real creation, power and possession. During one of his walks in Algabal's dead garden his thirst for life, his thirst for creation in life, broke out in a desperate cry:

How could I grow you in the holy ground,
Dark, big, black flower?

IV

No, the *fin de siècle* æstheticism with its worship of barrenness was not what George, possessed by his dream to see the beautiful, healthy, radiant body of his vision in flesh, wanted. His own glorification in the dark, arid, suffocating world of Algabal could not satisfy his need for light, air and fertility. Besides, his poems had begun to attract some companions around him and affect them in a strange and wonderful way. George began to realize that poetry is a power which can affect, influence, change human beings. He began to realize that his vision of a beautiful body could be made a tangible, warm, living, loving reality through the power of his verse. He began to realize that all his ambition, all his will to power, all his hunger for possession and leadership could be satisfied if he only used his poetic gift in the

6

right way. This thrilling discovery that poetry can attract, affect and give a definite shape to human beings, the discovery that poetry was not only a beautifully arranged refuge for weak and sensitive dreamers, but also a giver of life, a shaper of bodies, a creator of a new and more beautiful form of existence, made George free himself from the influence of decadent æstheticism with its sterility and look for inspiration in healthier, more luminous and fertile realms. The young poet became conscious of his new task, while he was still writing "Algabal." The last poem of this book showed what the poet's new direction was going to be:

> I saw big ravens fluttering,
> Black and dark grey crows,
> Near the ground over adders
> In bewitched fields.
>
> I now see swallows flying again,
> A snow and silver white swarm,
> How they balance themselves in the wind
> In the cold and clear wind.

His new series of poems were "Hirten- und Preisgedichte"— poems of a cold and clear day in which beautiful naked or half-naked bodies with a definite, emphasized contour, but without any individual features, walk about in a slow, ceremonial and classicist way. George had found himself. That was the kind of poetry that could bring into life the dream of the body he was longing to create and possess as a tangible reality. George was a man for whom the sense of touch was of the utmost importance. For him a human being was a being that could be touched—a body. Reality meant tangibility to him. All the world of the intangible things—of the soul, of the pure mind—did not exist for him. For him the soul was another word for the body:

> Did not the Sage teach: Prefer the beauty of the soul
> To that of the body?—"Body, soul, are only words
> Of a changing reality. The state grew rotten
> And the citizen shallow and impudent. Then the godlike one
> Devised the soul for help and salvation. . . .
> Not long ago you told us of the former friend:
> His clear eye grew dull, his flowering mouth dry,
> And his large forehead narrow. I do not know
> If you described the body or the soul."

This need for the tangible was so strong in George that it sometimes made him jealous of the sculptor who can create really tangible bodies with his art. "It was an unhappy morning," George made his poet Arcadios write to the Emperor Alexis—"it was an unhappy morning that led me to a statue by Lysippos which represents the God of wine and joy and which stands in a part of the garden I had not discovered before. It is true that the best works of this sculptor which I had seen in the capital, and some of which adorn your sublime residence, had filled me with amazement and admiration: yet I never before had found symmetry, strong limbs and delicate curves united in such a really godlike way, and Lysippos' art seemed to me to be the greatest gift of the Gods, in comparison with which all other gifts—even mine—would be slight and imperfect. Although I thought I heard Polymnia's and Erato's mild reproaches, and the memory of your kind praise, O Alexis, was an encouragement again: it was my first day of tears in Malakoi Potamoi." This feeling of frustration must have lasted until the poet realized, and he did realize it in the most vivid way, that the bodies of heroes created by sculpture are cold, motionless and of no use to the lover, while the bodies created by poetry are warm disciples made for action and love.

From the moment that George realized this the only purpose of his poetry was to attract and make such disciples. Later on he once confessed that he spent all his youth "dancing and playing the horn and the flute"—that is, writing the kind of poetry he wrote—not for the pleasure of it, but because this attracted gifted and beautiful young men around him.

Stefan George was still at the beginning of his poetic career when what we would call today spiritual fascism woke up in him. With his "Hirten- und Preisgedichte," he was already preparing his way towards leadership over a circle of devoted disciples. These poems were an appeal to young men to be beautiful, strong and real, and proud of their beauty, strength and reality, to recognize the Leader and be happy and proud to devote themselves completely to him. We do not know any other poetry in which the "leader principle" is taken up over and over again with such indefatigable persistence. Almost all human beings we meet in George's poetry are either the Master, the Leader, the Prophet, the Hero, or the Disciple, the Follower, the Believer, the Soldier, the Citizen. The poet ignored all other

human relationships. The only thing that mattered to him was
to make the young men who interested him believe that the best
thing they could do was to recognize him as their Master and
Leader, as if there was no love, no friendship, no intellectual
intercourse between equals in the world. No one has ever
depicted so temptingly as George the bliss of the disciple whose
only aim in life is to serve the Master:

> You talk of pleasures I do not desire,
> My heart is burning for my glorious Lord,
> You know the sweetness, but I know the fire,
> I live for the most glorious Lord.

In spite of such alluring descriptions of the pleasures one
would have if one became his devoted disciple, it seems that
things were not going very well for the Master and his circle.
Some of his friends had deserted him and he had had to break
with some others. Besides, even those who had stuck to him
could not satisfy him as completely as he wanted. He had to
recognize that he had failed up to now to find or create the friend
he needed. When he was approaching his thirties the feeling of
frustration and loneliness became so strong that he had to create
an imaginary friend—the Angel of the "Vorspiel"—with whom
to talk. The Angel was the person of his old dream, the person
he longed to meet in life or become himself. With the Angel he
could talk about his solitude, his despair, his doubts. He could
even discuss his disciples with him:

> And those who touched my knee full of devotion,
> And those I lead with only hints and nods,
> And those whose head has rested on my breast?

But the Angel's answer was only the cry of his own despair:

> The pupils love but are not strong and brave.

Actually the Angel was nothing but the poet's solitude. It was his
own loneliness that was speaking to him:

> You make me tremble out of pity; really,
> Besides yourself and me, you have not one.

And as time passed this solitude and despair were becoming
more and more unbearable, threatening the poet with destruction, until, as the legend goes, the miracle happened.

V

Unfortunately we do not know much about this miracle. George did not like people being inquisitive about it. What he wanted us to know about it he wrote down well concealed behind flourishes and falsities of style. His biographers avoid revealing more than the poet himself revealed; they usually quote his own words and keep their own thoughts to themselves. The whole story is presented like a myth, a legend stripped of all human interest.

The facts are that George met a boy in the street and that a passionate friendship developed, which did not last long, because a little while later the boy died. These were the facts, but George made a myth out of them, based a religion upon them, and this is how he spoke to the world about them:

"When we first saw Maximin in our town, he was still a boy. He came towards us from the triumphal arch walking with the unerring steadiness of a young fencer and the countenance of a powerful general, yet softened by that sensitivity and melancholy which were given to the faces of the people by centuries of Christian education. In him we recognized the embodiment of the omnipotent youth we had dreamed of, with its unbroken richness and purity, which even to-day moves hills and walks on the waters with dry feet—a youth that could receive our heritage and conquer new empires.

"We followed him and remained in the wake of his glory for days, before we dared to speak to him; but from the moment we spoke to him he accompanied us in our paths by his own will and without surprise, as if he was only obeying a law. The better we came to know him the more he reminded us of our ideal and the more we revered the extent of his unspoiled mind and the emotions of his heroic soul as well as their expression in his appearance, his gestures and his language.

"His nature moved even the insensitive common people: they waited for the time he would pass by to have a look at him or to listen to his voice. This voice was particularly moving—especially when he praised or defended someone or something, or when he read poetry to us and astounded us with a new magic of sound. Then the light brown colour of his skin would become purple and the way his eyes shone made us lower ours. But even when he did not speak or do anything, his mere presence was enough to make everyone feel the fragrance and warmth of a body really alive. We willingly gave up ourselves to the changing power which, with only its breath or touch, can give a virginal glow of paradise to everyday surroundings.

"All our thoughts and acts were transformed after this really godlike youth entered our circle. The oppressive reality of the times lost its exclusive might over us, since it now had to take a different direction. The peace which enabled each of us to find his own centre and the courage to throw away the confused burdens and to sink into the all-embracing sea was restored to us. We felt how futile all conflicts of the countries, all sufferings of the castes became before the stirring dawn of the great new day; we felt how all burning social questions faded into unsubstantial darkness when after each era a Saviour is revealed to man. . . .

"After these days of ecstasy he passed from a fever dream into death—so quickly that we only could stare at an ordinary grave without being able to believe that it was hiding him. We fell down in the blind despair of a brotherhood abandoned, we writhed at the meaningless, torturing thought that we could never more touch those hands, that those lips could never more meet ours. Then his living voice penetrated into us and made us feel our foolishness for wanting to keep him here by force, it made us understand the iron law, according to which early departure and highest nobility are inseparable. He also ordered us to stop our selfish tears and sobs and woke us up to the new existence which we had to begin with him. He now stands before us as we saw him for the last time: not in the icy merciless majesty of death, but in the victorious glory of the feast, adorned and with a wreath in his hair, not the image of a retired, enduring resignation, but of smiling and flourishing beauty. We now can eagerly, after impassioned signs of veneration, erect his statue in our sanctuary, kneel before him and worship him, as we were prevented from doing by timidity as long as he was still among us."

VI

This extraordinary document throws much light, not only upon George's nature, but also upon the nature of the German in general. George was now firmly following the tradition of his own country. The long and desperate need of the German mind for a new myth and a Messiah that would bring about a new epoch and a new order in world history made George give a mythical, a cosmological meaning to his friendship with a boy he met in the street. This friendship, as it seems, had had a cosmological meaning for George's private world. There must have been something complete and deeply moving in this relationship, and we would have been grateful to George if he had described it to us in all its truth. But unfortunately George did not speak about his friendship with Maximin with all the sincerity we would want. The document we quoted above is so extraordinary, because of the strange mixture of sincerity and insincerity, of candour and calculation, of truth and falsity, we find in it. When, for instance, George describes the warmth which Maximin's body radiated all round it, we are moved by the candid description of the lover's emotions at the presence of the beloved. But when he implies that this warmth was not only felt by himself, but that it had an objective power which was going to affect the whole world and bring about a new era of life, we cannot quite follow him. In a similar way when the poet says that Maximin revealed the essence of God to him, we can follow him, because the beloved moves us in a religious way and we could not be denied the right to worship him as a symbol of Divinity. But we would certainly be ludicrous if we tried to establish the person we love, and who is in some way a symbol of God to us, as God. And that is what George did. With the mind confused by a whole tradition of messianic expectations, needing badly a God who would consecrate him as a Leader and Master over the world, without the least sense of humour that would have protected him from such dangerous ways, deceiving himself as well as others, Stefan George made a God of his Maximin and appointed himself as the intolerant prophet of the new religion.

The prose piece about the life and death of Maximin, from which we quoted above, was the last thing which George wrote with some sincerity. After this he never wrote anything that could reveal his personal life. He only wrote what a prophet, free from human weaknesses, would write. The friendship with Maximin, instead of making the poet less rigid, mellower, more human, gave him an unheard-of confidence in himself and in the power of his poetry, increased his ambition to an incredible point and sent him out to the world with the determination to become the spiritual leader and shaper of mankind. He no longer was the poet speaking to a limited circle of congenial minds, he was the legislator of a new spiritual state.

Stefan George is an interesting poet, because his later poetry is the typical example of what we would call state poetry.

But what is state poetry? I think that in order to describe George's poetry we must explain what we mean by state poetry.

VII

Poetry, as we said, is a power. It can affect, influence, change human beings; it can give them a shape, a contour, or destroy the shape, blur the contour they have; it can make them act in this or that way, or even remain passive in life. Poetry has this power not upon all human beings, of course; it can affect only some of them, sensitive to its magic. Nevertheless, its magic is magic for them, and one could use poetry as a power upon them. A power that could make them either tread real, solid and strong upon earth, or " fade far away, dissolve, and quite forget." Human minds could be changed by the power of poetry into something as real and tangible as a body, or into something as unsubstantial as a shadow, a sigh, a cloud or a note of music. When we read Vaughan, Keats, Verlaine, Virginia Woolf or Rilke, and we are really sensitive to their magic, we give up our concrete, tangible existence to become something as vague and intangible as "an air of glory," the song of a nightingale, a sob, the paths of silence, the unfathomed mine of a soul. When, on the contrary, we read Homer, Whitman or George, we feel more dense, strong and solid than ever.

There are two kinds of poetry. The one gives more certainty, more solidity to our existence, the other dissolves it. This never passes unnoticed by the leaders or theoreticians with totalitarian tendencies. If a certain kind of poetry could be an extremely useful means in their hands for changing the people of their states into citizens and soldiers as they want them, there is another kind of poetry that could be a great danger to them. It frightens them and they have to fight it. That is why Plato, who knew better than anyone else what the power of poetry could do, turned the poets out of his state. In a state that needs the strong and well-trained bodies of citizens and soldiers there is no place for a poetry that could change one into a being of dream. One could imagine a monastery, but not a state populated with sighs and shadows. The culture of the state is the cult of the body—especially the body of the man. The woman is respected as the mother of strong and beautiful sons; but what we find in the centre of state poetry is the strong and beautiful body of the man. The poet has to worship it and respect it or go out of the state. One of Plato's reasons for turning Homer out of his republic was that the poet showed little respect for the hero's body when he described Achilles in a moment of extreme suffering distorting the dignified serenity of his appearance with spasms and gestures unbecoming to a man.

The verse of state poetry must not be intoxicating, like Keats' verse, for instance. It must not be too musical, because music makes one drunk, and drunk people cannot submit themselves to the state discipline. Its sound must be hard. Soft bodies, like soft poetry, have no place in the state. The verse of state poetry must be more like an inscription on marble than a tune lost in the air. It must have a definite contour as bodies have. It must be strict like army discipline. It is not allowed to wander in free rhythms like an individual with an inner rhythm of its own. All the characteristics of state poetry as we described it are to be found in George, especially in his later work. He is the most typical example of a pure state poet in modern times. Plato would never have thought of throwing him out of his state. And that is perhaps one of the reasons why George's poetry is so very little known in England. State poetry has never been cultivated in this country. It is true that Blake and Shelley knew that poetry is a power which could give a new legislation to a country, but they never thought of using it for changing their readers into soldiers and disciplined citizens.

By all this we do not mean that English poetry is a power dissolving the reality of man. On the contrary, we find a strong tendency in the tradition of English poetry to make man conscious of himself and his fate—that is, to make him more solid, more real. But the means English poetry uses to achieve this are different from the means used by state poetry. Instead of reconciling man with the world, the great English poets reveal to him the terrifying abyss of human destiny, they lead him to the verge of the precipice, and it is by the terror before nothingness that they make man more solid. The threat of utter destruction makes man gather all his forces in order to assert himself, his reality, his solidity against the powers of nothingness. The reader of English poetry may be

> re-begot
> Of absence, darkness, death: things which are not.

That is the power hidden in the greatest moments of English poetry, in Shakespeare and some of the Elizabethans, in Donne and other metaphysical poets, and that is what could have been achieved by T. S. Eliot if his conception of life was not so negative. We also find it in one or two of the young poets of today. Think of Stephen Spender's "Light and Darkness," for instance; and it is from a prose poem published a little while ago that the following lines, steeped in the best English tradition, were taken:

> No, not too much of the presence of death: not enough. I appeal to death, let him grant more dignity, more honour in our days.
> My advice to you when death shows his face, only twenty inches away?—Think of life.

VIII

George, as a typical state poet, wanted to worship life, light and the body, ignoring death, darkness and nothingness. Suffering, which distorts the majestic serenity of the body, was hateful to him even before he became a conscious state poet:

> It does not become us, born for the purple,
> To be shaken by earthly laments,

he said during his "Algabal" period. And later on, after he had left a friend to go to death by himself:

> I hated the useless ways of darkness.

As if the ways of darkness were ever useless and as if it was not out of them that our life draws its light. George's mind was too much of one piece to understand the dialectic mystery of existence, whose reality is born of nothingness, whose light comes from darkness, whose greatest hope is brought about by utmost despair. That is why when Maximin died what George tried to do was to forget the ugly realities of death, to conceal them behind a curtain of deceitful beauty, to make the grave invisible under a heap of flowers. George thought that by this he showed strength and courage, the strength and courage which eliminate the disturbing aspect of reality; but what he really showed was weakness and cowardice, the weakness and cowardice which do not dare to face the destructive, and because of that, by reason of something that our reason cannot grasp, the only really creative powers of existence. The bodies of soldiers and citizens must be always prepared to fight other, more tangible enemies than the "things which are not." That is why the state poet must put limits to the world and never speak of the enemies lurking beyond it, never speak of the unspeakable. In order to make his disciples stay within the limits of what can be spoken, George told them that "where the word breaks, everything ends." He also told them that they should never try to understand the incomprehensible. What he recommended them to take as a pattern, as an example for their lives, was the body—"die göttliche Norm," as he called it—the body with its tangibility and limits, its concreteness and contour, which do not transcend what is here and now and which could not get lost in the infinite. That is why George had to give a body to God, or rather to make a God of the body. It was only by this that he could keep himself and his disciples within the bounds of a limited and tangible world. But in this creation of a new myth there is something spurious. Hölderlin in a moment of mad despair, in order to bring a new tangible God into the world, arrayed himself as a Greek God, and in the middle of the night with a candle in the hand left his room to walk about the house where he was staying as a guest. He gave his hosts the fright of their lives, but his mad gesture had a moving, a tragic meaning, because it was spontaneous and desperate. But in George's myth-making there was neither spontaneity nor real despair. George needed a new God who would establish him as a Master and Leader over a circle of followers, and, deliberately, using the power of his poetry, he made the myth and preached the new God that would serve his plans so well. And he was successful. Some of his followers left him when they saw him becoming the prophet of a God he had created himself for obvious reasons, but others followed him, and many new, especially young enthusiasts, whose minds were prepared to accept something like that by the long messianic German tradition, were joining them. George was becoming the Leader of a new spiritual state. From now on his partly satisfied ambition became boundless. Since he had been able to create a new God and become the leader of a numerous following, what could stop him from becoming the Master, if not of the whole world, of Germany at least, which for a German is more or less the whole world? He called his circle of disciples "secret Germany," and prophesied to them that the "incomprehensible miracle of today"—the miracle that such a Master and such a circle existed —was going to become "the destiny of tomorrow." In his circle of disciples George saw the kernel round which a "new Reich," a new, beautiful, powerful and victorious Germany—the work of his own hands—would be formed. He told them that God's path was open to them, that His land was allotted to them, that His war had broken out for them, that His crown was theirs, that His peace was in their hearts, that His strength was in their breasts, that His anger was on their brows, that His desire was in their mouths, that His girdle was encircling them, that His bliss was given to them. He gave them an unfathomable conceit. He tried to make them forget that they were human beings— that is, unprotected, forsaken, helpless creatures, whom no one could save from suffering, failure and death. But no one can forget this with impunity. In spite of the conceit which they displayed in the streets, the George people were not more protected and helpful than other human beings. They only were more inhuman than people usually are. They were taught to despise failure and misery, to ignore death and nothingness, and it is only those who respect the mystery of failure and misery, those who are aware of death and nothingness, who can understand life. The George people were denied too many of the fundamental experiences given to man to be able to complete themselves. They remained half-blind beings walking on the brink of an abyss they were forbidden to see. The love that had created them must have been incomplete to have made them so incomplete. The poetry that had fashioned them, in spite of its power, which we cannot deny, since it created life, must have been spurious to have made them so inhuman. Its poet was one of those who prepared the way for the Nazis.

A LECTURE ON PROUST

(Translated from the French version by John Lehmann.*)

THERE are few things as tedious as those lectures or books which
have as their title "The philosophy of such-and-such a poet, or
such-and-such a novelist." In spite of that, in spite of not wishing
to be in the least tedious, I want to talk to you this evening about
the philosophy of a novelist—about the philosophy of Marcel
Proust. The title is not very promising, and I am sure you are
expecting something quite shattering; for that reason I hasten to
tell you that I shall endeavour to keep as far as possible from
everything the title suggests and you anticipate. And I shall do so
not only because I do not want to bore you, but chiefly because I
believe that what is customarily presented as the philosophy of a
poet or a novelist has nothing at all to do with philosophy; for
if it had, it would not be tedious. No doubt you think this is only
a paradox; but one of the most common misconceptions is the
idea people have about the nature of philosophy. They think of
it as an abstract and useless science that has nothing to do with
life—with *our* life—and that when it enters our experience in
the guise of a lecture or a book can only make ordinary healthy-
minded people yawn. Almost everybody has this idea about
philosophy, even those who are at pains to discover the philosophy of their favourite poet. They read the poet's work, they
make a note of the most abstract passages, and then with these
passages and using their own thoughts to fill in the gaps they try
to construct a system, which they present to us as the philosophy
of this author or that author. Of course, this construction is as far
removed from true philosophy as it is from the author to whom
it is attributed: God forbid that I should behave in such a
manner to an author of whom I am so fond as Proust. But the
better to avoid making such a mistake, I would like to say a few
words about what I believe true philosophy to be. I do not
believe that philosophy is a science—far less an abstract and useless science that has nothing to do with life, with *our own life*.
The study of the works of the great philosophers teaches us the

* The quotations from C. K. Scott-Moncrieff's translation of Proust are
made here by kind permission of Messrs. Chatto and Windus.

complete contrary; and in order to give you an idea of what these works do teach, in order to show you that philosophy is very far from being something abstract, boring and alien to our life, I shall choose as an example a philosopher who has the reputation of being very abstract, very boring and very dry—I shall choose Aristotle. There is a little phrase of his, hidden away in one of his least-read works, which may help us to understand the true nature of philosophy. "Being," says Aristotle, "is better than not being, it is better to be alive than not to be alive." Of course it is better to be alive, you will say, than not to be alive! We need no philosophy to tell us what everyone knows so well. And yet, reflect again. Does everyone really know what true life is? Is it not possible that there are people who might maintain that not being is the only kind of existence that is worth while, and that death is better than life? Let us take the poets. Take, for instance, Shakespeare. Listen to what Claudio says in *Measure for Measure*:

> To sue to live, I find I seek to die;
> And, seeking death, find life . . .

Remember also the words of Iphigenia in Goethe's play:

> A useless life is nothing but a premature death . . .

Even La Fontaine, the La Fontaine who wrote the *Fables* and whose life was so varied and so delightful, even he complained at the end of his career that in spite of his life as a "butterfly of Parnassus flying from flower to flower and from object to object," he had not really lived. In spite of the richness of his life, he did not consider it a true life. I could quote many other examples; but what they all make us feel is that the nature of true life is not as obvious as one might think, and that certain people a little different from the ordinary are aware of this and try at all costs to discover and to realize the kind of life that is worth being lived. These people, a little out of the ordinary, are the true philosophers. They are in search of being, as Aristotle would have said—and it is to this search that Proust devoted his life. His long novel called *In Search of Lost Time* could very well have been called *In Search of Being*. In any case even his actual title is sufficient indication that this search for "lost time" is nothing but the search for real being. We have no need to look for Proust's philosophy in occasional chance reflections, scattered here and there in the text, which it would be extremely difficult to assemble into anything like a system. His thought, not in the least rhapsodical, was the continuous movement of his reason inflamed by his passion for existence. Like nearly all the great philosophers, he was neither dogmatic nor a maker of systems. His mind was always in movement, always searching, always experimenting. To quote Aristotle again: "Philosophy is for ever occupied with a question which has no answer." The momentary solutions that one finds for a problem have only significance for the moment. The important thing is the *continual movement*; and it is that which constitutes the philosophic life, and that which Proust makes known to us in the sixteen volumes of his novel. But before considering this work of Proust's we ought to know something about the life and personality of the author. Behind all philosophies there are living men, whose expression they are. Even the most frigid speculations are the product of a human life, very often the product of an unique suffering. Proust's philosophy makes such a deep impression on us because it was the expression of a suffering the depth and intensity of which make us shudder.

I do not know if we will ever come to learn the concrete facts of Proust's life which led him to despair. Although his immense novel is nothing but one long confession, we do not know precisely what Proust suffered, nor what people made him suffer, nor whether it was friendship or love—and if love, what kind of love—which brought him the greatest disappointments. He himself said: "No one wishes to unlock his soul." And in spite of the revelations which he made about himself, which surpass in audacity and sincerity all previous confessions in history, he managed to conceal from us what he was really like. Henri Massis, whose recent study shed the most revealing light yet.on Proust's inner life, goes as far as to assert that the aim of his life, of his art, of his deepest impulse, was to prevent himself "from being recognized, identified, discovered." Even his most intimate friends who have published their recollections of him—either because they do not want to say too much or because they do not really know very much—never tell us enough. His letters tell us even less. We know nothing of the love affairs of a man who has spoken to us so much about love.

Marcel Proust was born in Paris in 1871, and was the son of a professor of medicine and of a cultivated Jewess with frail health. His love for his mother was the most important fact in Proust's life. One could plausibly maintain that the final aim of his work was to show the unique importance of the relations between a mother and her son. His health was very delicate, and from earliest childhood he had to give up many things which he loved —the open air, the smell of trees, the scent of flowers, which suffocated him. He had an almost pathological sensibility. His ardent imagination, his refined taste, and perhaps a need to forget himself, made him fling himself eagerly into the worldly life of the titled aristocracy, whose names inflamed his imagination, and of cultivated society, whose manners enchanted him so often. That is why we find people asserting that he was the perfect snob. But we should not forget that snobbery is a way, like any other, of forgetting oneself, of assuaging one's suffering. Apparently, during the first years of his worldly life, Proust had some dark disappointments and sufferings. The little volume of stories, poems, dialogues and thoughts which he published in 1891 under the title of *Les Plaisirs et les Jours* reveals this clearly enough. The stories in this volume, in particular, are the confessions of people who have known the darker places of vice, who have felt a horror of them and have suffered the consequences. It seems that Proust plunged ever deeper into the emptiness of worldly life in order to lose himself and to free himself from the terrible visions which pursued him. And what was worse was that he had to lie to the only person in the world who meant anything to him: to his mother. That mother died, and Proust saw with horror that he had let her go without giving her any of the things she expected from him. Perhaps it was this remorse which made him decide to retire from the world, and create the great work which he could but feel that the dead mother he loved so much still hoped for from him. So it was that he lived during the whole of the last part of his life, an ascetic's life, remote from the world, sleeping during the daytime and working at night, in a room sealed from the noises of the outside world, with Céleste, the faithful servant whom he immortalized in his novel under the name of Françoise. Paul Morand, who was in close contact with him during that time, has written a poem in which he describes Proust and the atmosphere of the room in the house on the Boulevard Haussmann where he lived in creative solitude. That *Ode à Marcel*

7

Proust gives us the most vivid impression of Proust during those days, a creature of the night and solitude, whose despair was only half hidden under the half-ruined mask of a man of the world.

Thus, in that atmosphere of modern asceticism—for Proust was a true ascetic in spite of his experiences of the underworld—in that rather sombre atmosphere, and with an almost incredible concentration of effort, he produced his great work, sixteen volumes which form an indivisible whole. I prefer to call it a "work" rather than a "novel," because it is not a novel in the strict sense of the word, nor simply an autobiography, and one certainly cannot call it a book of science or pure philosophy. Works which express the whole personality of an author cannot be exactly classified. That is why we can examine Proust's work from the most different points of view. We can talk of Proust's psychology, Proust's sociology, Proust's æsthetic, or, as I am doing at the moment, of Proust's philosophy. And I believe we certainly have the right to talk of philosophy in connection with Proust. It is not because I am particularly interested in philosophy that I have discovered it in Proust's work. No; as I said earlier on, even the title of his book is evidence of preoccupations which Aristotle could only have described as philosophic. There is a certain passage where Proust has described the way in which he composed his book, and which ends with an incontestable avowal of his philosophical passion. I think if I read you that passage it will be the best way of passing from the biographical part of this lecture to the part devoted to his ideas. Any writer worthy of the name (says Proust) must shut himself up in a kind of darkness, because all great works are the children of darkness and silence; he must shut himself up for years together and prepare his book with the most minute care, "with continual regroupings of his forces as if for an offensive, endure it as if it were a duty imposed upon him, accept it as a rule of life, build it like a church, follow it like a prescribed régime, overcome it like an obstacle, win it like a friendship, feed it like an infant and create it as if it were a world, mindful of those mysteries the explanations of which are probably only to be found in other worlds, the intimations of which move us more than anything else in life and in art."*

Those mysteries, which Proust mentions in this memorable

* *Time Regained.*

passage, are nothing but the problems which create a philosopher. They have no answer—they can perhaps be explained in other worlds—but when they present themselves to us they are so overwhelming that the only point of our lives can be to find a solution. And when we think like that, we are in fact coming back to what Aristotle said about philosophy, that it is for ever occupied with a problem which has no solution. This problem presents itself to us under many guises. Each of us has his own special way of seeing it and experiencing it. And that is why it is so interesting to be acquainted with all the different philosophies, or rather with the thought of all the different philosophers. Each philosopher has his own individual way of experiencing the problem, which is different from everybody else's way. The influences which come from outside are in most cases only superficial, limited to language and form. There has been too much talk of the influence of Bergson and Ruskin on Proust. My own belief is that Proust changed what he took from them to such an extent that there is not much point in stressing their influence. One thing, however, which has been absolutely ignored is the resemblance of Proust's philosophy to that of an English poet— to Wordsworth's philosophy. The central experience in the famous "Ode on the Intimations of Immortality from Recollections of Early Childhood" is one of the principal motifs of Proust's work. In that famous poem Wordsworth tells us that during his childhood—

> meadow, grove and stream,
> The earth, and every common sight
> To me did seem
> Apparell'd in celestial light,
> The glory and the freshness of a dream.

But he then goes on to tell us that the "visionary gleam" has fled and the dream has faded away—

> The things which I have seen I now can see no more.

In spite of this, he tells us that these recollections of childhood are a "perpetual benediction" and the "fountain-light" of all his days, which—

> Uphold us, cherish, and have power to make
> Our noisy years seem moments in the being
> Of the eternal silence: truths that wake
> To perish never . . .

The things of the external world are, for the child, symbols of a truth which is not to be understood, but only felt. The grown man can no longer see such symbolism in the world around him, and it is for that reason that he must call on his memory to re-create what he saw during his childhood, and to feel once more the depth beneath the appearance of things.

One must admit that such an experience is by no means common to everyone. There are some writers who cannot bear the memory of their childhood, who hate their childhood: André Gide, for instance, or Thomas Gray. There are, however, others —such as Wordsworth, Vaughan, Hölderlin and Proust—who find the most solid reality in their childhood, because it speaks to them of the mystery of another world. In order to re-create his childhood—or rather the sense of intimacy with the mystery of the world which his childhood gave him—Wordsworth wrote his *Prelude*. For the same reason Proust wrote his great novel. His years of childhood were for him, in his own phrase, "les terrains résistants sur lesquels il s'appuyait," and that because in those recollections of childhood he saw the true symbols of the mystery of existence. But how was he to recover their special quality? Ordinary memory cannot re-create the symbolic nature of things. Luckily, according to him, there is a kind of involuntary memory which, with the aid of the things themselves, can recover contact with their symbolism. "I feel there is much to be said," he wrote, "for the Celtic belief that the souls of those whom we have lost are held captive in some inferior being, in an animal, in a plant, in some inanimate object, and so effectively lost to us until the day, which to many never comes, when we happen to pass by the tree or to obtain possession of the object which forms their prison. Then they start and tremble, they call us by our name, and as soon as we have recognized their voice the spell is broken, we have delivered them; they have overcome death and return to share our life. And so it is with our own past. It is a labour in vain to attempt to recapture it, all the efforts of our intellect must prove futile. The past is hidden somewhere outside the realm, beyond the reach of the intellect, in some material object (in the sensation which that material object will give us), which we do not suspect. And as for that object, it depends on chance whether we come upon it or not before we ourselves must die."*

* *Swann's Way.* Translation by C. K. Scott-Moncrieff.

It was on just such an object, and its miraculous power, that Proust built up the whole edifice of his novel. That object was a little cake called "madeleine," which his mother gave him one day with his tea. In the taste and smell of the "madeleine" Proust recovered his lost childhood. While he was still a child his aunt gave him the same cake when he went to see her in her room. And now, "just as the Japanese amuse themselves by filling a porcelain bowl with water and steeping in it little crumbs of paper, which until then are without character or form, but, the moment they become wet, stretch themselves and bend, take on colour and distinctive shape, become flowers or houses or people, permanent and recognizable, so in that moment all the flowers in our garden and in M. Swann's park, and the water-lilies on the Vivonne and the good folk of the village and their little dwellings and the parish church and the whole of Combray and of its surroundings taking their proper shape and growing solid, sprang into being, town and gardens alike, from my cup of tea."* That evocation of the past, or rather that resurrection of the past by means which are not intellectual but almost magical, is the principal aim of *A la Recherche du Temps Perdu*. The philosophic significance of such a resurrection is clear, because it is the resurrection of the symbols of a truth which affects us without our being able to define it. But it is not only the living recollections of our childhood which have this particular quality. We are always meeting people and things which disturb us in the same way when they present themselves to us as individual realities. One of the greatest enigmas which tortured Proust, which made up the joy and agony of his life, was the enigma of the *individual*.

Proust believed that everything in life which is general—a general idea, one person like another, for instance—is of far less importance than the individual, than what is unique in the world, what cannot be replaced or represented by anything else. He believed that pessimists are only pessimists because they see happiness as something generalized. But happiness is never generalized. Happiness always comes in some unique shape; it is always new, always unexpected. We can never tell in advance what will make us happy. That is the reason why those who believe in what is unique, individual and unexpected believe

* *Swann's Way*. Translation by C. K. Scott-Moncrieff.

also in happiness. Apart from what is individual, everything is empty, denuded of interest and desperately boring. One might perhaps maintain that such thoughts are nothing but the ideas of an æsthete. But with Proust individuality is not merely something æsthetic: it is the very essence of things. It is the force which, in love, causes our peculiar emotion about the beloved. Nor is it the perquisite of people alone. Even inanimate objects can, by the force of their individuality, become unique and irreplaceable for us. According to Proust, there is a feeling which turns things from a mere spectacle to beings *without any equivalent*. Even landscapes (he says) have a certain quality of individual life. Even a room has its individual charm. The belief that certain things have an individuality of their own can give to those things a soul which they keep, and which grows in us. The *name* of a thing is generally the beginning of such a development of individuality. When he was young, Proust tells us, "I did not think of towns, landscapes, historic monuments as more or less agreeable scenes, cut out here and there from the same material, but I thought of each one as an unknown being, essentially different from all the rest, which my soul craved to know, and would have much profit from knowing. And how much more individual they became when they had names, names which only existed for them, like the names of people. Names give us an image of people—and of towns which they accustom us to think of as individual, as unique as people—a confused image which draws from them, from the brilliant or sombre quality of their sound, the colour with which it is uniformly painted, like one of those posters, completely blue or completely red, in which, owing to the limitations of the process employed or a whim of the artist, not only the sky and the sea are blue or red, but also the boats, the church, the passers-by. The name of Parma, one of the towns I most wanted to visit since I had read *La Chartreuse de Parme*, seemed to me compact, glossy, mauve and tender; if anyone talked to me of some house in Parma where I should be received, the pleasure it gave me was to think that I should live in a glossy, compact, mauve and tender house which had no connection with the houses in any other town of Italy, because my imagination pictured it with the aid of that heavy syllable of the name of Parma where no air circulated, and of all I had made it absorb of Stendhalian sweetness and the reflected gleam of violets. And when I thought of Florence the image that sprang up before me was of a town miraculously embalmed and like the corolla of a flower, because it was called the city of lilies and its cathedral Sainte-Marie-des-Fleurs."* Proust found it impossible to choose between those two towns, both of which had for him so incomparable an individuality. Neither could ever replace the other for him. But generally the names of people and of things are too narrow. They make the things they stand for seem too simple. One nearly always fills the name of something unknown with fancies, dreams. And this dream-content rouses in us the desire to know the thing or the person more intimately. And that is very important, because Proust tells us that without such a desire we can never know anything. If one desires something one wants to possess it, and knowing it is a way of possessing it. But the individual personality of another person is not something one can possess, it is not something that one can know. Individuality is something irrational, something our reason cannot grasp. We can only desire it, move in its orbit, struggle, sacrifice ourselves, even die for it. This struggle for what is individual reaches its purest and clearest expression in love. What makes the person we love so mysterious, so desperately desirable for us, is his or her individuality. When we find in someone only general concepts, we cannot love that person. Love begins when we begin to see in another person something individual, something unique and without any equivalent. Then it is that every movement of that person, even the most trivial, and every gesture appears to have an importance, a significance, that is terrible in our eyes. We suddenly have a strange new awareness. The existence of the person we love in the world we generally find so boring gives it a miraculous beauty. We watch the rising of the sun of one of our beloved's glances as if it were some wonderful spectacle, and we examine the growth of a smile as if it were a phenomenon of nature. But love is by no means satisfied with such wonder and admiration alone. According to Proust, love is the insensate and intolerable desire to possess the beloved. Not merely physically: physical possession is not really possession at all, said Proust. One wants to possess the whole being of the beloved. It is an old truth, and we find it in Plato's *Symposium*, in the speech of

* *Swann's Way.*

Aristophanes when he says that "what the lover wants of the person he loves is something indefinable, that one can feel but not express." Proust, like a philosopher who wants to express the inexpressible and find the unfindable, cannot be satisfied with such a statement. He wants to find the meaning of love at all costs. He cannot rest content with the usual solution which is given to the problem of love. He refuses to be deceived, even by himself. He will have nothing to do with the idea that procreation is the real point of love. To look for its true meaning he had the courage to leave the regular paths of love to descend into the accursed towns of Sodom and Gomorrah. This is not the time or place to follow Proust in that terrible descent which is one of the most overwhelming things in literature since the descent of Dante into Hell. What we know is that Proust has depicted the suffering and sterility of love in a quite terrifying way. And what is worse is that, in spite of all that he dared to risk, when he asks himself, What is it that binds us to the person we love? What is it in love that we must possess or die? he finds no answer. But Proust cannot endure that. To escape that suffering, that philosophic anxiety that is always looking for something it cannot find, there is only one way: to lose oneself in the general, to forget oneself in objectivity and the calm of natural laws. It is in this mood that he formulates those general laws of love, and tells us that suffering is the universal and inevitable fate of lovers. He tells us that love is a kind of madness, and he never tires of repeating it. He even reaches the point of denying his deepest belief, in saying that individuality—which, as we have seen, has a far greater reality and importance for him than anything else—is nothing but an illusion. "What we call individual," he says, "is merely something general." It is with such remarks, general, objective and detached, that Proust seeks to escape from his anguish, from his intolerable suffering. And he did it deliberately, as an ailing doctor gives himself a drug. It is he who said that "life, love and suffering lead us to dead ends." But those walls that life puts up across our path can be pierced by the intellect. The intellect does not recognize any closed situations in life, from which there is no issue. With the intellect one can dissolve the person one loves into a vaster reality—so vast that one might be able to forget that person. One might be cured of the suffering of love, if one pretended to oneself that it was a kind of illness—an illness, for instance, of the heart.

There are moments in Proust's work when the need to find a solution in philosophy of the most urgent problems of existence is so painful that we begin to feel that we cannot go on, that we must put the book down. We summon our intelligence to our aid, to give us a moment of rest, of respite; but only a moment, because philosophic anxiety can never cease, can never allow us to stop for good. Proust's affirmation, for instance, that love is only a kind of madness and the individuality of the person we love an illusion, has nothing definitive about it. We turn the page, and we find Proust fighting with all his strength to find another solution to this problem that in reality has no solution. He has changed his point of view. He tries to avoid ever being the same. It is the surest way to avoid the danger of dogmatism. The only thing we find is constant with him is anxiety—always bound up with the preoccupation caused by the problem of time. The abstract problem of time—what time is apart from our individual life and our suffering—is not so overwhelming as the problem of the relation of our own life to time. We might say that time is ourselves. Our "I" is not something static, inflexible, always the same. Our "I" is a movement in time—that is, a perpetual process of change. But normally we are not aware of our movement in time. We consider ourselves as something fixed. The greatest tragedy in life, says Proust, is that our heart changes. But we only know it through our imagination and through novels. We know perfectly well the theory that the earth revolves, but in reality we take no account of it. We walk on something which appears motionless, and we live in peace. It is the same with time. It is for that reason that novelists, to make us really feel the passage of time, accelerate the speed of events in a quite frightening way, and in two minutes hurry us through ten, twenty, thirty years. It was through novels that Proust had his first revelation of the fact that he was not situated *outside* time but *in* time, and there was nothing he could do about it. That first revelation, so full of sorrow, is presented to us in his novel in a most remarkable way. One of the chief aims of *A la Recherche du Temps Perdu* is to make us feel time as something living, inseparable from our own existence. When we come to the end of the sixteenth volume, to the end of the novel, the new idea of time we have acquired makes us feel giddy. Proust gives us a new awareness of ourselves, the awareness of our existence in a fourth dimension, the dimension of time. This new awareness is certainly dangerous. When one feels oneself so bound up with time, when one feels oneself so completely its prisoner, then despair is not far away. Proust's novel would indeed be a work of absolute despair if one did not find in it the great belief which was Proust's sole support: the belief in art. He believed that art could liberate man from the prison of time. His reasons for that belief are of no great interest. They were invented by faith. But could one say that Proust found a definitive solution to the problem of life—the solution of art? No; I believe that, in spite of that faith, Proust never ceased to ask himself the philosophic question, the question that has no answer. It was in one of his moments of most complete sincerity that Proust wrote that "art can show us what riches, what enormous variety is hidden in the night of our souls—the night of our souls which we call nothingness." It was in another such moment that he asked himself whether nothingness is not indeed the truth and all our dream nothing but a lie.

Nothingness—everything—called God by believers—are the two names which philosophers give to the darkness which surrounds our existence. The true philosophers are those who can make us feel this thing that some call God, and others nothingness. And that is why we find in Proust a true philosopher. He is always talking to us of nothingness, of the darkness of our soul and the night which extends beyond our lives: the night which those who believe call God.

DOSTOEVSKY

I had a dream where in a cave all night
With some protean shape he could not see
A creature with a face of human woe
Wrestled: and that night was eternity.

I

"I CANNOT regard Dostoevsky as a good or happy man," somebody
who knew the Russian novelist well said once of him: "He was
bad, debauched and full of envy. All his life long he was a prey
to passions that would have rendered him ridiculous and miserable had he been less intelligent or less wicked. In Switzerland,
in my presence, he treated his servant so badly that the man
revolted and said to him: 'But I too am a man!' I remember
how I was struck by those words . . . addressed to one who was
always preaching sentiments of humanity to the rest of mankind."

But did Dostoevsky ever preach any sentiments of humanity
in his creative work? It is true that there are passages in it which,
if they are read in isolation, sound like sermons exhorting men to
love one another and have faith in God. But it is also true that
there are other passages in it which, if they are read in the same
way, sound like exhortations to inhumanity, or like blasphemies.
If Dostoevsky is human as a writer, it is not because he preached
feelings of humanity, but because he showed, in the most disturbing way, how questionable all human values are. If he is a
religious writer, it is not because he preached faith in God, but
because he showed with an unequalled power how questionable
all faith is. These remarks may sound paradoxical, but I hope
that in the course of this essay I shall make clear what I mean by
them.

Dostoevsky is a writer full of contradictions, and he can be
described only in a paradoxical way. He is human, because he
dared to face the extreme limits of inhumanity, and religious,
because he went as far as nihilism can go. His thought is so disturbed and disturbing because his life made him realize, like
Job, that there is no hedge round man's existence protecting it
from the powers of nothingness.

We are told in the Book of Job that when once God prided

Himself to Satan on the "perfection and uprightness" of a man on earth, Satan remarked: "Hast not thou made an hedge about him, and about his house, and about all that he hath on every side? . . . But put forth thine hand now, and touch all that he hath, and he will curse thee to thy face."

There are two kinds of writers: those whose world is protected by a hedge, and whose truths are unambiguous, and those whose world is not protected by anything against the powers of nothingness, and whose truths are bound to be ambiguous, since, for them, there is no line of demarcation between the things which are and the things which are not. Jane Austen is a typical example of the first, Dostoevsky of the second group of writers.

II

Round every page of Jane Austen's novels one feels the hedge of an eighteenth-century English home. It is the hedge of "sense," of logic, or rather of the logic of a person leading a secure life in the midst of a secure society. Jane Austen was protected by a hedge of unquestionable values; she could always tell the right from the wrong, a noble from a mean character. Even when the evening of her life came, and, as we see in *Persuasion,* she realized with a shiver she tried to conceal that all hedges surrounding one's life are bound to vanish in the approaching darkness—even then, in the twilight, she could still distinguish baseness from nobility with as much self-confidence as ever. "Mr. Elliott," she could write, describing baseness of character as if she knew all about good and evil, "is a man without heart or conscience; a designing, wary, cold-blooded being, who thinks only of himself; who, for his own interest or ease, would be guilty of any cruelty, or any treachery, that could be perpetrated without risk of his general character. He has no feeling for others. Those whom he has been the chief cause of leading into ruin he can neglect and desert without the smallest compunction. He is totally beyond the reach of any sentiment of justice or compassion. Oh, he is black at heart, hollow and black!" That is how one can judge and condemn "baseness," evil in human nature, when one lives secure in a circle surrounded by a protecting hedge. Then one can afford to play the part of a sensible, sensitive, self-confident and dignified judge.

But to others it appears that such a part is based on an illusion, and that no one can be really secure in life. Behind even the most solid-looking hedges there are terrors lurking which, sooner or later, break into one's life to shatter one's logic and make one's values questionable. It is so pleasant to read Jane Austen because she gives us the illusion that there are no such terrors, and that if we take good care of the walls protecting our home, no burglar, no murderer can ever break in to disturb our sleep. Those who do not like to feel that this is an illusion had better keep off Dostoevsky. Because Dostoevsky is, above all, the writer who lived and created unprotected by any hedge, and whose work destroys in his readers' minds the illusion that there can be any security in life. "Do you really think," he wrote to one of his admirers about the end of his life, "that I am one of those who save the hearts, who free the souls, and who drive suffering away? Many people write this to me, but I think that I am much more able to inspire disillusionment and disgust. And, above all, the feeling of insecurity."

Dostoevsky's famous houses with their narrow, high, and steep staircases leading into complete silence and darkness, are not surrounded by protecting walls; they have no locks for keeping evil out. Burglars, murderers, and all kinds of evil-doers, ghosts, and even Satan himself, break in at any moment of the night or the day, and the most atrocious crimes, the most disturbing scenes, the most destructive discussions take place in their rooms, stuffy with obsessions, smelling of blood. In these houses even the purest love proves murderous, even the deepest faith blasphemous. In their rooms one cannot very well distinguish the right from the wrong, what is noble from what is base. "Oh, what is base a man understands particularly well! But was it base? How can a man judge?" asks one of Dostoevsky's characters, the narrator of *A Gentle Spirit,* at a moment when he sees all the hedges protecting man from utter despair collapse for him, leaving him alone and helpless in the middle of a hostile world.

A Gentle Spirit, a short work as disturbing as any of Dostoevsky's long novels, is the story of two people who, although they meant everything to one another, could not help torturing one another to such a point that one of them was driven to suicide. The other, unable to grasp how he could be responsible for the death of the person that was everything to him, can only stand in the middle of a world empty for him, and cry railing at the torn pieces of all hedges set up by society, religion, logic, or nature round man's life: "What are your laws to me? What do I care for your customs, your morals, your life, your state, your faith! Let your judge judge me, let me be brought before your court, let me be tried by jury, and I shall say that I admit nothing. The judge will shout, 'Be silent, officer.' And I will shout to him: 'What power have you now that I will obey? Why did blind, inert force destroy that which was dearest of all? What are your laws to me now? They are nothing to me.' Oh, I don't care! . . . Oh, blind force! Oh, nature! Men are alone on earth— that is what is dreadful! 'Is there a living man in the country?' cried the Russian hero. I cry the same, though I am not a hero, and no one answers my cry. They say that the sun gives life to the universe. The sun is rising and—look at it, is it not dead? Everything is dead and everywhere there are dead. Men are alone—around them is silence—that is the earth!"

III

This experience has been often described by Dostoevsky. All his most important works were carefully planned to lead to descriptions of this experience. Dostoevsky, as his whole work testifies, had a strong feeling of insecurity all his life long. And it was natural: he was always in financial difficulties; he was always ill; he was often betrayed in love; he himself had often to be unfaithful; he was guilty, perhaps, as some people suspected, of terrible crimes; his life must have been a constant reminder that no hedge can protect one from the powers of destruction threatening to break into one's life at any moment.

But apart from his insecurity in everyday life, Dostoevsky experienced in his late twenties something so terrible that one finds its memory behind everything he wrote afterwards. I mean the famous scene on the scaffold of Semyonovsky Square. Everyone knows the facts: When Dostoevsky was twenty-eight he was arrested as a member of a secret revolutionary society. He spent eight months in prison, and after he was tried, one morning he was taken, with nineteen other prisoners, to Semyonovsky Square, where the death sentence was read to them. Everything seemed to have been prepared for their execution: the scaffold was erected; the soldiers who would shoot them, and the priest who would confess them, were there; Dostoevsky was even shown a line of coffins ready to receive their bodies. The procedure started: they were given the cross to kiss, the sword was broken over their heads, and they were dressed in funeral white shirts. Three of them were already standing against the pillar, and Dostoevsky thought that he had only one more minute to live, when suddenly the procedure of the execution stopped and they were told that the Emperor had reprieved them. It was all a fake, only meant as "a lesson they should never forget."

From that moment on Dostoevsky lived only in order to remember the metaphysical "lesson" given to him by this experience. It was said by some critics that this experience does not seem to have played an important part in Dostoevsky's later development, since he seldom mentioned it or alluded to it in his writings. But no one likes to recall the scenes whose terror has left the deepest impression on one's mind. On the contrary, one tries to forget them. Their terror is always present in one, and one's mind is full of the terrible knowledge they left behind them. I have the feeling that, in some way, the most stirring parts of Dostoevsky's work repeat under various forms the revelation which the writer had that morning on the scaffold of Semyonovsky Square.

"Who can tell if human nature is able to bear this without madness?" Dostoevsky wrote later, when protesting against the death sentence and describing the horror of the certain death, in one of the few places in which he alluded to his terrible experience. "Why this hideous, useless, unnecessary outrage? Perhaps there is some man who has been sentenced to death, been exposed to this torture, and has been told, 'You can go, you are pardoned.' Perhaps such a man could tell us. It was of this terror and of this agony that Christ spoke, too. No; you can't treat a man like that!"

But Dostoevsky was treated like that, and he did tell us under the most various forms and in the most disturbing way what the man knows who faced death from so near and without any hope of escape. "Do you know," he wrote many years later, about the end of his life, "what fear of death actually means? He who has not been near death can hardly imagine it." Dostoevsky's experience on the scaffold is one of the main obstacles which make his work so difficult to understand. Even the most daring thinkers, unless they have had an experience like Dostoevsky's, cannot go, by their thought only, as far as Dostoevsky went. Those whose life has never been invaded by devastating terrors will never quite understand why Raskolnikov murdered the old woman, why Stravrogin married Marya Timofyevna, or even why a "breath of corruption" should come out of the coffin where Father Zosima's body lay.

"What most people regard as fantastic and lacking in universality I hold the inmost essence of truth," Dostoevsky said once. The fantastic aspects of things attracted him even before the terrible experience of Semyonovsky Square, as his youthful story *The Double* shows. But the fantastic nature of "the inmost essence of truth" must have been revealed to him in a complete and unforgettable way while he was realizing what the death sentence read to him meant, or rather while he was realizing how meaningless this death sentence was.

To the man who knows that in a few minutes he is not going to exist any more because of something terrible whose meaning no reason, no sense of justice, no sense of order, can grasp—to such a man the world must indeed appear as something fantastic. At such a moment he will look round and will not recognize the world he used to know. He used to believe in values, in logic, in order, in all the things which make a connected whole of the world; he used to feel protective hedges all round him; but suddenly the world appears as a boundless void, in which no values, no meaning, no order, can have a place. He is lost in the middle of a "fantastic" emptiness. The man who longed with all his being for an unquestionable meaning, is "insulted and downtrodden" by the endlessness of the meaningless void. "No; you can't treat a man like that!" is the cry of those who suddenly experience the fantastic nature of the inmost essence of truth. And that was Dostoevsky's cry.

IV

But this "fantastic" nature of truth is revealed not only during some rare moments of extreme spiritual terror. We can also experience it in everyday life if we are involved in something connected with values which mean everything to us—in love, for instance.

Dostoevsky's love life is a long, complicated and "fantastic" story. In order to show what kind of truths it must have revealed to him, I shall say a few words about its most characteristic chapter, the writer's relationship with his first wife, Marya Dimitrievna.

He met her while he was serving as a soldier in a Siberian battalion, soon after he had been released from prison, and he fell passionately in love with her. She was then the wife of a tubercular customs official, but she did not rebuff him. What her response really meant, if there was any disinterested feeling in it at all, I cannot say. The whole relationship is a problem, and a very sordid one at that, I am afraid. Anyway, the first chapter of the story soon came to an end; Marya's husband was transferred and she had to leave the place where Dostoevsky was stationed. "I have lost what meant everything to me," the writer wrote to a friend in despair. Yet, after a few months Marya's husband died and she was left in poverty with a son. Dostoevsky, who was poor himself, helped her with money as much as he could, while she was having an affair with a young schoolmaster. Her new lover wanted to marry her, but the prospect of a life of extreme poverty did not appeal to her, and she preferred to marry Dostoevsky, who, in the meantime, had been given a commission, and who, as a writer, when he would return to European Russia, would have more possibilities to give her a more or less comfortable life. And she did need a more or less comfortable life, because after they left Siberia she became tubercular herself. They lived in Tver at first and then they moved to Petersburg, but the climate of this town had a bad effect on Marya's chest and her husband sent her back to Tver. There the second ghastly scene of Dostoevsky's life took place. His sick wife, who had just been abandoned by her lover, the schoolmaster, who up to then had followed her from place to place, in her despair and exasperation, told her husband that she had never loved him—"how could a woman who respects herself love a man who spent four years in prison in the company of thieves and murderers!"— and that she had been betraying him all the time. Dostoevsky, deeply hurt by this, not only in his feelings, but in those depths where the physical, the emotional and the spiritual roots of existence are inextricably interwoven, started an affair with a young girl. The lovers went abroad together, where Dostoevsky was be-

8

trayed by the girl. He returned to Russia, to his sick wife, who, a few months later, died.

That is the outline of his sordid love story. But in love stories dry facts do not tell one much; one must know what the facts meant to the lovers, how the lovers lived the facts. After Marya Dimitrievna's death, Dostoevsky wrote a letter to a friend in which we can see what, in spite of the facts, his relationship with his first wife meant to him: "Oh, my friend! She loved me immensely, and I loved her as much; nevertheless, we did not live happily together. I shall tell you all about it when we meet; I only say now that, although very unhappy together (because of her strange, hypochondriac and morbidly bizarre character), we could not stop loving one another. On the contrary, the more unhappy we were, the more we loved one another. It may seem strange, but it was like that. She was the most truthful, the most noble, the most generous woman I have ever met." In another part of this long letter Dostoevsky expressed his decision to remain faithful to her memory.

His wife had died in April, 1864; this letter was written in March, 1865. A year later he was in love again, with his secretary, whom he married in February, 1867.

V

Love was the highest of all values for Dostoevsky: "The chief thing is to love others like yourself, that's the great thing, and that's everything; nothing else is wanted," he wrote once. Love, he believed, was the only thing which could make man happy. Yet, as we have seen, love did not give happiness to Dostoevsky in his relationship with Marya Dimitrievna. "The more unhappy we were, the more we loved one another," he wrote, as we have seen; and it would have been equally true if he had reversed the sentence and said: "The more we loved one another, the more unhappy we were." Love may be the highest of all values, but it can also become one of the most negative and repulsive manifestations of life. "I have gone so far," says the hero of *Letters from the Underworld*, who, as somebody who knew the novelist well remarked, was not unlike Dostoevsky, "as to arrive at the firm conclusion that, properly speaking, love lies in the peculiar right of tyrannization which the fact of being loved confers. Even in my most secret soul I have never been able to think of love as aught but a struggle which begins with hatred and ends with moral subjection." In life love is closely connected with hatred, and perhaps no one has shown this terrible truth more convincingly than Dostoevsky. He had experienced this truth in his own life, as we know, and throughout his work the problem of this "fantastic" truth is always present: "In my hatred for the men of our earth there was always a yearning anguish: why could I not hate them without loving them? Why could I not help forgiving them? And in my love for them there was a yearning grief: Why could I not love them without hating them?"

Love, and not only love, but everything which could give a meaning to our life, is ambiguous. It can be something positive, creative, human, but another time, or even at the same time, this same thing can be negative, destructive, inhuman. Nobility of character can be closely connected with meanness, creation with destruction.

Man, who needs something unambiguous, unquestionable, to hold on to, discovers, to his despair, that no ground is absolutely safe in life. Love might suddenly appear as hatred or as indifference, life as death, freedom as enslavement, creation as destruction, as if everything were making fun of man. One is not certain even of one's own self, even of the unity and the unambiguity of one's own personality. "Do you know, I feel as if I were split in two," says Versilov in *A Raw Youth*. "Yes, I am split in two mentally, and I am horribly afraid of it. It's just as though one's second self were standing beside one; one is sensible and rational oneself, but the other self is impelled to do something perfectly senseless, and sometimes very funny; and suddenly you notice that you are longing to do that amusing thing, goodness knows why—that is, you want to, as it were, against your will; though you fight against it with all your might, you want to." The second self standing beside one, the "double," was one of Dostoevsky's favourite themes. One is so divided that one does not know what is oneself and what is one's double. One of Dostoevsky's early works, written even before the experience of Semyonovsky Square, is the story of the humiliations and insults inflicted upon a man by his own double.

Man is lost and helpless in a world in which everything is ambiguous, in which everything, even his own self, appears as something else. How can one save one's pride and keep one's dignity in a world where everything seems to make fun of one? How can one understand the meaning of all this? "Too many riddles weigh man down on earth," says Dmitri Karamazov. "We must solve them as we can and keep a dry skin in the water." The trouble is that one cannot do it. One gets wet, and one feels "humiliated and injured," hopelessly ridiculous in the middle of endless insulting puzzles and ambiguities. I think that the best introduction to Dostoevsky's thought is his short story *The Dream of a Ridiculous Man*.

VI

A stimulating writer, the Russian Leo Shestov, said that we must look for the real *Critique of Pure Reason*, not in Kant's work, but in Dostoevsky's *Letters from the Underworld* and the great novels which followed them. I think that Shestov has not been quite fair to Kant, but, at the risk of being unfair myself, I would say that the real *Discours de la Méthode* is to be found in *The Dream of a Ridiculous Man*.

Both Descartes' essay and Dostoevsky's short story have the same subject. They deal with the way in which truth may be revealed to the man who begins by doubting if there is any truth at all in the world. But, curiously enough, while Descartes' *Discours* is considered as one of the most important philosophical works the human mind has ever produced, Dostoevsky's short story, which no "History of Philosophy" has ever mentioned, as far as I know, is much more philosophical. Descartes' doubt is not a real one. When once the French philosopher found himself in a strange town where he had nothing better to do, he liked to spend his days in perfect comfort sitting by the stove and amusing himself with his own thoughts. There the germs of a thought started growing in his mind, of the thought that in order to find truth one should begin by pretending "that everything which ever entered one's mind had no more truth in it than the delusions of one's dreams." But that is only a pretence of the mind, not the real doubt which confronts one's whole being with nothingness. This real doubt was described by Dostoevsky in *The Dream of a Ridiculous Man*. The "ridiculous man"—or rather Dostoevsky himself, because it is quite clear that in this

short story Dostoevsky described a personal spiritual experience
—does not pretend that nothing exists in order to amuse himself
while he sits comfortably in a well-heated room. There are no
walls, no hedges protecting the ridiculous man from the terrors
of life. Ever since he was a child he remembers nothing but
insults and humiliations—not only from other human beings, but
from the nature of existence itself. "I went to school," he says,
"studied at the university, and do you know, the more I learned,
the more thoroughly I understood that I was ridiculous. So that
it seemed at the end as though all the sciences I studied at the
university existed only to prove and make evident to me as I
went more deeply into them that I was ridiculous." Man comes
into the world with a will of his own, but nothing obeys his will,
since everything has to conform itself to the laws of nature,
which seem to laugh at man's deepest needs and aspirations. The
deeper one goes into science the more conscious one becomes of
one's impotence and of the futility of one's will. But it is not only
science which makes one feel ridiculous. "It was the same with
life as it was with science," Dostoevsky goes on. "With every year
the same consciousness of the ridiculous figure I cut in every
relation grew and strengthened."

Man, Dostoevsky knows, is helpless and pathetic in his struggle
to find an unquestionable value to hold on to in life. Every time
he grasps at something, this something, whatever it may be, always
proves to be something else, often its opposite. All really important things in life are protean in shape, and with every change of
their meaning they seem to be laughing at man. Man is deeply
wounded, and if he is sensitive enough, he must, sooner or later,
ask himself if there is any meaning in life at all.

The conviction that *"nothing in the world matters"* comes suddenly upon the ridiculous man. "I suddenly felt," he says, "that
it was all the same to me whether the world existed or whether
there had never been anything at all: I began to feel with my
whole being that there was *nothing existing*. At first I fancied
that many things had existed in the past, but afterwards I guessed
that there never had been anything in the past either, but that it
had only seemed so for some reason. Little by little I guessed that
there would be nothing in the future either."

This nihilism "felt with one's whole being" is something real
and might lead to discoveries of real truths; in comparison with

it, Descartes' "feigned doubt" seems unreal, and, certainly, if it can lead to anything, it must be to something which does not matter. Descartes' doubt does not really concern one's existence; it is harmless; it can neither save nor destroy one. Dostoevsky's nihilism, on the contrary, is dangerous, because it concerns one's whole being, and if it can reveal truth, the meaning of life, it can also destroy one. It can lead to suicide.

When the "ridiculous man" came to the conviction that nothing mattered, he decided to kill himself. He did not do so, because by chance something suddenly happened to him which made him see the truth that there are things in life which matter. But if it had not been for this chance he would have committed suicide, like that other nihilist Dostoevsky created, Stavrogin. One must read Stavrogin's letter in the "conclusion" of *The Possessed* to see where nihilism felt with one's whole being may lead. "I know I ought to kill myself, to brush myself off the earth like a nasty insect," we read in this letter; "but I am afraid of suicide, for I am afraid of showing greatness of soul. I know that it will be another sham again—the last deception in an endless series of deceptions. What good is there in deceiving oneself? Simply to play at greatness of soul? Indignation and shame I can never feel, therefore not despair." In spite of that, Stavrogin did commit suicide.

The "ridiculous man" also would have killed himself, if on his way to his lodgings, where he was going to carry out his plan, "a shuddering and shivering all over" little girl, who was in distress for some unknown reason, had not cried to him for help "with that note in her voice which in frightened children means despair."

What made the ridiculous man realize that there is something in life the existence of which one cannot doubt was, not the irrelevant thought *that one thinks*, Descartes' famous *je pense donc je suis*, which does not lead anyone anywhere, but the cry of despair of a helpless human being.

VII

If one tried to build a system out of the various thoughts Dostoevsky expressed about life, one would fail. It is true that in his works all the most important problems of human existence are discussed, and that in them one finds fascinating aphorisms about life and death, good and evil, God and nothingness. Yet these aphorisms never express Dostoevsky's static views. Dostoevsky did not have any static views. As we saw when we quoted some of his aphorisms on love, Dostoevsky could give the most contradictory answers to the same question. And this is natural, since, as we have seen, everything seemed protean in meaning to Dostoevsky. Since everything in the world is ambiguous, a thinker true to himself must not be frightened of contradictions. "Oh, you two-penny-halfpenny philosophers and wise men! Why do you stop halfway?" asked the hero of *Crime and Punishment*, but that is what Dostoevsky himself might have asked. Integrity and courage of thought were so important to him that as a thinker he never stopped halfway. On the contrary, he went so far in thought that most of the time he was standing on the verge of nihilism.

The only thing which is never ambiguous or questionable in Dostoevsky's work, and which saved Dostoevsky's thought from nihilism, as it saved the "ridiculous man" from suicide, is the cry of despair of a helpless human being.

The reality of this cry cannot be questioned. The fact of human suffering and not the belief in unquestionable values is what makes Dostoevsky's philosophy so positive. Dostoevsky questions all values and has often to confess that he does not believe in them, but the more one doubts them, the more distinctly one hears the cry of human despair. The emptier the world seems to be, the more real the existence of man appears. That is what makes Dostoevsky's work so human. It is full of inhumanities, yet in an inhuman world the protesting voice of humanity fills the void.

This voice might be turned against the world as it is, as it happens in *A Gentle Spirit*; it might be turned against logic and reason, as in *Letters from the Underworld*; or might be turned even against God, as in Ippolit's confession in *The Idiot,* or in *The Grand Inquisitor*.

Dostoevsky, as we said, was not one of those thinkers who would stop halfway. The history of philosophy is full of examples of thinkers who, instead of letting themselves and the others go so far as to accuse God because of the way man is treated in the world, tried to find reasons by which to justify Him. In philosophical jargon this effort of the human mind to justify God is called "theodicy." But theodicy is an effort to stop one's thought at halfway. Those who dared to go to the end of the way, instead of justifying God, accused Him, and Dostoevsky was one of them.

His work is a long trial at which God is being judged, but which cannot come to a verdict. Man cannot condemn anyone; he cannot be certain of anything apart from his own suffering. The only thing he can do is to protest, but, as Ippolit says in *The Idiot*, "a protest is sometimes no small action." Certainly a protest as powerful as the one heard throughout Dostoevsky's work is an action of great importance. Those of his readers who can hear it may be reminded by it that the more questionable everything appears, the more unquestionable the truth of something in man's existence, revealed by suffering and the awareness of nothingness, becomes.

NOTE.—The passage from Strakhov's letter quoted at the beginning of the essay I took from Gerald Abraham's *Dostoevsky* (Duckworth). The quotations from *A Gentle Spirit, The Dream of a Ridiculous Man, A Raw Youth, The Brothers Karamazov, The Possessed, The Idiot,* are from Constance Garnett's translations (Heinemann). Those from *Letters from the Underworld* and *Crime and Punishment* are from the translations in Everyman's Library (Dent). For the quotations from Dostoevsky's letters I used J. W. Bienstock's French version (Mercure de France). I also used S. Koteliansky's *Dostoevsky Portrayed by His Wife* (Routledge). I strongly recommend Janko Lavrin's excellent *Dostoevsky* (Methuen). The motto of the essay is from John Lehmann's *Poem for Two Voices*, published in *The Listener*.

THOMAS GRAY AND HORACE WALPOLE

(A chapter from an unfinished study)

GRAY went up to Peterhouse in October, 1734. His first impressions were not encouraging. He arrived with a feeling that he was not going to belong to the place. The *terra incognita* in which he found himself frightened him. His innate fearfulness made him suspect hostility everywhere, and he stood on the defensive. Instead of allowing himself to receive all that this new life could give, he shut himself up and shunned all contact with outside. But that is not the right attitude for one who wants to take part in life. Gray, thirsty for life, found himself shut in the silence of his own room—a silence suggesting emptiness, sterility, death. "You will not find it strange," he wrote to Walpole three weeks after his arrival in Cambridge, "that I don't go abroad, when I tell you that I am got into a room, such a hugeous one, that little i is quite lost in it, so that when I get up in the morning, I begin to travel towards the middle of it with might and main, and with much ado about noon bate at a great table, which stands half way it: so then by that time (after having pursued my journey full speed) that I arrive at the door, it is so dark and late, and I am so tired, that I am obliged to turn back again: so about midnight I get to the bedside: then, thinks you, I suppose, he goes to sleep: hold you a bit; in this country it is so far from that, that we go to bed to wake and rise to sleep; in short, those that go along the street, do nothing but walk in a sleep; they run against every post they meet; but I beg pardon of talking so much of myself, since that is not what you care for. . . ."

These phrases mean much more than at first appears. They reveal not only humour, wit, nonsense, caricature, to amuse the friend; they are rather the cryptic but unmistakable expression of Gray's inner life. His despair, projected into the external world, distorted the forms of things to his eyes and made a nightmare of reality. If we visit Gray's rooms in Peterhouse, without knowing much of his life in Cambridge, we do not suspect anything nightmarish in them. They look like the other Cambridge College rooms made for study, for social intercourse and for rest. But for him they looked quite different; they were his own place as endless as the despair, as empty as the sterility and as unreal as the unreality of his life. His description of his room we have read is not a whimsical, but an exact expression of what he saw in it.

One can say the same of his descriptions of Cambridge and of Cambridge people and life. The distorted, frightening picture he gave of them was the picture of his own fears, his anxiety, his inferiority feelings—not an objective account of what the place actually was. When I said that his first impressions of Cambridge were not encouraging, I did not mean that Cambridge itself was discouraging. They were mere symptoms of Gray's despair.

When, as we already know, he described the people in the streets of Cambridge walking about in sleep, he only wanted to express how unreal was his own life, how unreal Cambridge was to him, and how far away from him he felt all its people—as if they lived in a world where no contacts were possible. When, again, he compared Cambridge to "a spider with a nasty lump in the middle of it, and half a dozen scrambling legs"; or when in one of his letters he put as a headline, "All is dust, all pie and all tobacco" (in the colleges, of course), he did it because Cambridge and his college were the place of his despair to him. The images he used to describe them were drawn out of his own soul, which, like other desolate places, was full of spiders and their webs, of "ghostly rats," of dust and of unpleasant smells—the usual brood of desolation. He once dated one of his letters "from St. Peter's charnel-house." He knew that he was a dead man in life. But Peterhouse was none the less a place of youth, for all that.

Those who see in Gray's impression of Cambridge a document of solid historical value make a serious mistake. Eighteenth-century university life was often pictured in most lurid colours of debauch and ignorance. Some authors, in order to give an idea of this life, quote Swift's famous passage, in which Oxford and Cambridge are represented as places where young people "learn nothing more than drink ale and smoke tobacco," and they make it more convincing with one or more corroborative phrases from Gray's letters. The testimony of one as serious as the poet of the *Elegy* is unquestionable and the picture looks convincing. But we already know enough of Gray's Cambridge not to be taken in. We know that Gray's testimony does not represent anything objective.

If Gray had recognized the objective values of his milieu—

especially the social ones—he would have had to deny himself. He was nothing according to them. If in his milieu the phrase "This fellow never had a grandfather!" was an expression of utter contempt, Gray was not able to produce even a father. According to social standards he was nobody. But his morbid feeling of insecurity, his innate anxiety, made it a necessity to him to feel as though he was "somebody." Nothing would have persuaded him to associate with the other "nobodies" of the place. Friendship with them would have reminded him all the time that he was one of them. But what he needed was to regard himself as their superior and to think of them as of "these creatures, infinitely below the meanest people you could even form an idea of." To be again introduced into the circles of people with whom he would have liked to mix, because they would have made him feel "somebody," must have been extremely difficult, especially for one who was rather unattractive, awkward and dull in company. But that would not have been the main difficulty. "There was little to bring young men of different upbringings together, and much to keep them apart," writes the historian of eighteenth-century Cambridge. "Social prejudices were both stronger and more respectable than they are today, and a boy on coming to the University was not encouraged to discard them. He was, indeed, encouraged to observe them. He was admitted at a college and matriculated in the University either as a nobleman, a fellow-commoner, a pensioner or a sizar; and this division of undergraduates into classes, roughly indicative of their stations in life, must have emphasized class distinctions."

Gray was admitted at Peterhouse as a pensioner. The pensioners were the most numerous and the most mixed class of undergraduates. Among the great number of them who would not have been able to produce a father there were to be found a few younger sons of baronets. It was not so degrading to be a pensioner after all. It would have been too hard for his mother to bear all the expenses of Gray's education, so he was obliged to ask for scholarships. He was given two of them—the Cosin and the Hale—and as a scholar he had to comply with regulations concerning not only his studies and his behaviour, but even his appearance. He was not allowed to dress as the others did. At a time when the care of the hair was everybody's concern, he was not allowed to wear long locks and use hair powder. He had promised to avoid all extravagance of dress—and by "extravagance" much was meant that was the general fashion. He must have resented the imposed decency of his appearance. Although a pensioner, he could not present himself like the other pensioners; he must have felt almost like one of those wretched sizars, the really poor students, who were treated no better than servants. They had to wait at table and act as gyps to their more fortunate comrades.

Gray hated his real position in Cambridge, and he had to isolate himself and create an imaginary one. In his solitude he felt superior and he could despise all the others: "The fellows are sleepy, drunken, dull, illiterate things; the fellow-commoners are imitators of the fellows, or else beaux, or else nothing; the pensioners grave, formal sots, who would be thought old; or else drink ale and sing songs against the excise. The sizars are graziers' eldest sons, who come to get good learning, that they may all be Archbishops of Canterbury."

This contemptuous attitude made it possible for Gray to isolate himself in a dignified way, but it could not help him to fill the emptiness of his solitude. He had to spend his time with the dream he had of himself—the dream of himself as the intimate friend of the most charming, the most brilliant, the most influential young man of the time, "the most agreeable thing in nature," a favourite with the best London society, the son of the Prime Minister, whom all the noblemen and fellow-commoners of Cambridge would have been so flattered only to meet once: Horace Walpole.

Gray's feelings for his dear Celadon were more than friendly —we could even say more than passionate. Horace meant everything to him. He was the centre round which Gray's whole existence revolved. Without this centre Gray would have felt nobody —not only socially, but in a much deeper sense—lost, without any support, annihilated. He felt alive and real only as far as he could think of himself as Horace's friend: "The chain of destiny linked me unto thee, and the mark, which Gabriel stamped on my forehead at my nativity, was born for Miradolin," Gray wrote to his friend with a pathetic sincerity under a playful tone. "As your soul is large enough to serve for both of us, it will be ill-

natured of you, if you don't reanimate my corpse. . . ." But such a
friendship, such a union as Gray wanted it, can only—if at all—
be experienced in some rare moments; it is of a mystical, metaphysical, often deceptive order; we cannot be sure of its reality in
everyday life. But Gray's existence was dependent on it. In order
to feel like a living being and not like a "corpse," he had to feel
himself united to the friend. But this was not easy. How could he
be certain that Walpole was really his friend? After they left
school they did not see each other for a long time. Horace was
coming up to Cambridge as a member of King's, but he did not
seem anxious to arrive. He was living the fashionable life of his
father's circle, lost in a whirlpool of parties, balls, dinners, masquerades, masques, operas, plays—lost for Gray. They exchanged
letters, and Horace's letters were friendly indeed. But what
did this mean? Horace was just as friendly to all his friends,
and he had so many of them. He was so far, moving in
another world, and his friendliness seemed so remote, so inscrut-
able, so uncertain. It was too uncertain to make one whose existence rested upon it feel secure. Gray felt insecure, anxious. His
only hope was that when Horace came up to Cambridge the
miracle of security in their friendship would take place. In the
meantime he could only write letters to his friend, in which he
tried in a concealed but unmistakable way to reveal, to confess
himself—all his need, all his misery, all his passion.

In these letters he could only repeat again and again: "I am in
danger, help! I am in danger, save me!" We must not expect to
find anything else in them. We already know that Gray's impressions of Cambridge have no objective value. They were only
one of the ways in which he expressed the same thing, his friendship. "P. Bougeant," wrote Gray later, providing the key to inter-
pret the letters of the period we are describing now—"P.
Bougeant, in his *Langage des Bêtes*, fancies that your birds, who
continually repeat the same note, say only in plain terms, 'Je
vous aime, ma chère; ma chère, je vous aime'; and that those of
greater genius indeed, with various trills, run divisions upon
the subject; but that the *fond*, from where it all proceeds, is
'toujours je vous aime.' Now you may, as you find yourself dull
or in humour, either take me for a chaffinch or nightingale; sing
your plain song, or show your skill in music, but in the bottom
let there be 'toujours, toujours de l'amitié.' "

That is exactly what Gray did. He knew that if he had said in a direct and explicit way the only thing that mattered to him it would have sounded strange, impudent, humiliating, monstrous. Silence would have been the only answer he could have expected. The only possibility for him to say the only thing he had to say was to present it concealed under various disguises, all meaning the same. So he described, as we know, Cambridge as a place of despair, meaning: "Any place without you is a place of despair," or something like that. He described a party to which he was invited as nothing but stupidity, horrid "noise and disturbance," in order to add at the end of the account: "You will think it a strange compliment when I tell you how often I thought of you all the while; but will forgive me when you recollect that 'twas a great piece of philosophy in me to be able, in the midst of noise and disturbance, to call to mind the most agreeable thing in nature." He spoke of philosophy only to say: "The term is now begun again, and I have made such a wonderful progress in philosophy that I begin to be quite persuaded that black is white, and that fire will not burn, and that I ought not to give credit to my eyes or feeling; they tell me too that I am nothing in the world, and that I only fancy I exist: do but come to me quickly, and one lesson of thine, my dear philosopher, will restore to me the use of my senses and make me think myself something as long as I am your friend and servant." He wrote verses in a tone of parody in order to say things that he had to say, but which would appear ludicrous if expressed in another tone:

> When Celadon commands, what God had disobey?

> Believe that never was so faithful friend
> Queen Prosperine to Pluto underground,
> Or Cleopatra to her Marc-Antony
> As Orozmades to his Celadony.

The fancy-dress of a book like *The Turkish Spy,* a novel full of the most exotic images and the maddest passion, was precisely the thing needed by Gray. The extravagance of his passion could be safely presented as a pastiche of the most extravagant exoticism. But one must not be deceived by the wit of the parody. There is no phrase in this letter that is not a cry of despair:

"When the Dew of the morning is upon me, thy Image is upon my eyes; nor when the night overshadoweth me dost thou depart from me. shall I never behold thine eyes until our eternal meeting in ye immortal Chioses of Paradise: and sure at that hour thy Soul will have little need of Ablution in the sight of Israphiel, the Angel of examination: surely it is pure as the Snow on the Mount Ararat, and beautiful as the cheeks of the Houries: the Feast of Ramadan is now past away and thou thinkest not of leaving Candahar; what shall I say unto thee, thou unkind one? thou hast lost me in oblivion, and I am become as one, whom thou never didst remember: before; we were as two Palm-trees in the Vale of Medina, I flourish'd in thy friendship and bore my head aloft: but now I wander in Solitarinefs, as a traveller in the sandy deserts of Barca, and pine in vain to taste of the living fountain of thy conversation. I have beheld thee in my Slumbers, I have attempted to seize on thee, I sought for thee, and behold! thou were not there! thou were departed as the smoke or as the Shadows, when the Sun enters his bed-chamber: were I to behold thy countenance, tho' afar off, my heart would bound as the Antelope; yea! my soul should be as light as the Roe-buck on the hills of Erzerom. I swear by Abubekir, thou art sweet in my thoughts as the Pine-apple of Damascus is to the tast; and more refreshing than the fragrant breezes of Idumea. the chain of Destiny has linked me unto thee. . . . let not the demon Negidher separate us; nor the evil Tagot interpose between us. Be thou unto me as Mohamed was to Ajesha; as the bowers of Admoim to those whom the Sun has overtaken; or as the costly sherbets of Stamboul to the thirsty: the grace of providence, and the smiles of heaven be upon thee. May white Angels guard thee from the efforts of the rebellious genii."*

This letter was the most pathetic masquerade held during this time of mania for masquerades. In eighteenth-century England everybody—the people of fashion as well as the mob—was mad about this amusement. Gray was thrilled by the mere mention of it. He imagined himself in the midst of a masquerade protected by a disguise. The masque if it is tasteful—and Gray considered himself as a man of taste—conceals the inferior social position, the want of physical attractions. It can even disguise one's sex. Gray's position in his milieu was ambiguous, and only the deceit of a masque could have made him appear

* From the Oxford Press Edition of *The Letters of Thomas Gray* (edited by Toynbee and Whibley).

as he would have liked to have been—equal to the best, important, free, charming. Behind his masque he could have got rid of his inferiority feelings, his shyness, his inhibitions. He might have been run after, courted; he might have made a figure and enjoyed himself. If the world were a masquerade Gray might have been a success.

But he had no opportunities of going to masquerades. His only possibility was to hold private and silent masquerade in letters. Disguised in dresses taken out of wardrobes like *The Turkish Spy*, he could walk, dance, gesticulate in words with a greater freedom. He pretended to be amusing—as one has to be, if one is in fancy dress—but actually he was not amusing in the least; he only was his real self, expressing himself in desperate, often obscene gestures. He could not have been conscious of the meaning of all these gestures. No one can deliberately reveal so much of his secrets. Although Gray revealed so much, the revelation was well concealed under the masque. Perhaps even young Walpole did not suspect the truth. But today we cannot doubt any more. Even the parts of the last-quoted letter that seem to have a decorative character only, like the phrase at the end, "May white Angels guard thee from the efforts of the rebellious genii" —even such phrases have a definite and disturbing meaning. Thirty-five years later Gray wrote the same thing, this time almost undisguised, at the end of a letter to another friend: "Shall the allurements of painted woman *comme il faut*, or the vulgar carefses of prostitute beauty, the property of all that can afford to purchase it, induce you to give up a mind and body by Nature distinguish'd from all others to folly, idleness, disease and vain remorse?" The angels and the genii of the young man as well as the didactic tone of the old man reveal the same thing, the pangs of physical jealousy. In his relations to young Walpole, Gray experienced all the sufferings of unrequited love.

A VIEW OF ENGLISH POETRY

Let not our words be like flowers which are in the fields today and
tomorrow cast into the oven, not like flowers, even though in their magnificence they surpass Solomon's glory—KIERKEGAARD.

IF one could explain why the English are the gentlest and at the
same time the most stubborn people of the world, one could also
explain why the English language is the poetic language *par
excellence*.

The English are gentle and stubborn at the same time, because
they are neither too gentle nor too stubborn. Balance is the secret
of the English genius.

About three hundred and fifty years ago the Elizabethan poet
Michael Drayton (1563-1631) described the English genius in a
way which after all this time has lost nothing of its truth. The
genius of "Albion's glorious isle," he says, is the genius of a
place:

> Where heat kills not the cold, nor cold expels the heat,
> The calms are mildly small, nor winds too roughly great;
> Nor night doth hinder day, nor day the night doth wrong,
> The summer not too short, the winter not too long.

English is the creation neither of the day nor of the night
alone, but of both. That is why it can express the light as well as
the darkness of the soul with equal power.

English is the child neither of the body nor of the spirit alone,
but of both. That is why it can in one and the same poem be as
heavy and tangible as a perspiring body, or as light and insubstantial as a playful breeze. Both the following quotations are
taken from Ben Jonson's "Epistle to My Lady Covell":

>   a tardy, cold,
> Unprofitable chattel, fat and old,
> Laden with belly, and doth hardly approach
> His friends, but to break chairs, or crack a coach.
> His weight is twenty stone within two pound. . . . . . .
> The Muse is one can tread the air,
> And stroke the water, nimble, chaste and fair;
> Sleep in a virgin's bosom without fear,
> Run all the rounds in a soft lady's ear,
> Widow or wife, without the jealousy
> Of either suitor, or a servant by.

9

This is delightful poetry, but it is too well balanced to be great poetry. Drayton, who used the English language without disturbing the balance of its spirit, is a poet one admires and respects, but he does not disturb us in the way all powerful poets do.

Blake is delightful when he expresses the balance of the English genius, as in the lines:

> Joy and woe are woven fine,
> A clothing for the soul divine;
> Under every grief and pine
> Runs a joy with a silken twine.
> It is right it should be so;
> Man was made for joy and woe;
> And when this we rightly know,
> Thro' the world we safely go——

Blake, however, is powerful only when he disturbs this balance, tears the precious "clothing" protecting the soul, and does not feel safe any longer:

> The beggar's rags, fluttering in air,
> Does to rags the heavens tear.

All great English poets disturbed the balance inherent in the spirit of their language. Even Drayton said that "a poet's brain" should possess "a fair madness." Power in poetry begins with anxiety.

Even Chaucer, who seems to express the balance of the English genius more powerfully than any other poet, was not free of anxiety. It is true that he is "a poet of light," as Edith Sitwell says, and that the world he created is very much like the lovely room and day described in *The Book of the Duchesse*:

> And, sooth to seyn, my chambre was
> Ful wel depeynted, and with glas
> Were al the windowes wel y-glased,
> Ful clere, and nat an hole y-crased,
> That to beholde hit was gret joye . . .
> My windows weren shet echon,
> And through the glas the sunne shon
> Upon my bed with brighte bemes,
> With many glade gilden stremes;
> And eek the welken was so fair,
> Blew, bright, clere was the air,
> And ful atempre, for sothe, hit was;
> For nother cold nor hoot hit was.

The last two lines remind us of Drayton's description of the English genius. One does not see very well in which corner of this lovely room and in which fold of this festive day anxiety and fear could find a place. Yet Chaucer knew that the world of light he had created was only a fabric woven out of language, and that language is a fragile material at the mercy of time, moths, winds, human hands, minds and mouths. I think that the following address to his "litel book," *Troilus and Criseyde*, which expresses all his anxiety about the fate of his work, is one of the most moving verses in the language:

> And for ther is so greet diversitee
> In English and in wryting of our tonge,
> So preye I god that noon miswryte thee,
> Ne thee mismetre for defaute of tonge.
> And red wher-so thou be, or elles songe,
> That thou be understonde I god beseche!

Chaucer's bright day flutters like a torn flag in the wind of nothingness, if we think that although English has become the safest language of the world, the reality which Chaucer tried to preserve "with pitous herte" in his English has been almost "devoured out of memory" by that "elde" which "can frete and byte" everything.

While Chaucer was concerned with the durability of his work, the Scottish poets of the following century, more interested in the physical side of existence, were obsessed with the disintegration of man's flesh. Henryson (*c.* 1425-1500), in his *Testament of Cresseid*, shows how fascinating the poetry of the disintegration of the living human body can be, and Dunbar (*c.* 1460-1520) laments the physical death of the poet:

> He (Death) has done piteously devour
> The noble Chaucer, of makaris flour,
> The Monk of Bury, and Gower, all three:
> *Timor mortis conturbat me.*

As if the physical life of a poet mattered more than his poetry.

Who can say what is more real: a living human being or a "real" poem?

Man is either frightened of unreality and tries to become as real as possible, or weary of this reality and tries to become unreal.

"I hate both poetry and wine without body," said Landor; while we find in Webster:

> Do not weep:
> Heaven fashioned us of nothing; and we strive
> To bring ourselves to nothing.

Poetry is a power which can make us feel either as real and solid as a tangible body, or as unreal and insubstantial as a dissolving dream.

The body of the beloved is for some people the only tangible proof of their own existence.

Marlowe is the English poet who lives in his poetry not only as a spirit but as a body. His spirit is one with his body. His spiritual hunger is one with the hunger of his senses. He tries to embrace the absolute by pressing the whole world with all its treasures, and even what extends beyond the world, the unknown, in his arms. And it is not only he himself who exists in his poetry as a body. I do not know any other English poet who described the physical reality of others with such sensuousness as Marlowe in his verses:

> Even as delicious meat is to the tast,
> So was his neck in touching, and surpast
> The white of Pelops shoulder: I could tell ye,
> How smooth his breast was, and how white his belly;
> And whose immortal fingers did imprint
> That heavenly path with many a curious dint
> That runs along his back. . . .

Yet even Marlowe, who struggles in his poetry to become more and more tangible by embracing more and more tangible things, suddenly becomes weary of tangibility, of reality, and expresses the longing to bring himself to nothing:

> O soul be chang'd into little water-drops,
> And drop into the ocean, ne'er be found!

The Scottish poets of the fifteenth century tried to become real by showing the human body in its disintegration, Marlowe by singing its triumphant bloom; yet Marlowe expressed the longing to bring himself to nothing in a stirring way.

Keats is as sensuous a poet as Marlowe, but, unlike Marlowe, he used his sensuousness in order to dissolve his reality into an intense unreality:

> Fade far away, dissolve and quite forget
> What thou among the leaves hast never known,
> The weariness, the fever and the fret. . . .
>
> Verse, Fame and Beauty are intense indeed,
> But Death intenser. . . .

This death is not a real but an imaginary one. Keats, weary of his reality, tried to lose himself into an unreal death. Yet, just as Marlowe, who struggled to become as tangible as possible, in *Doctor Faustus* expressed his longing to be lost in nothingness, so Keats, too, who struggled to get rid of himself in an unreal world, stopped, frightened, in "Hyperion" to say:

> I am gone
> Away from my own bosom: I have left
> My strong identity, my real self,
> Somewhere between the throne, and where I sit
> Here on this spot of earth.

This "strong identity," this "real self," seems far away from the reality of the body. To be a tangible reality does not always mean to be one's real self. To stand firmly on a spot of earth does not always mean to be present there.

Nazi philosophy, the philosophy of *Blut und Boden,* identifies man's reality with man's body, and man's real presence with his firm stand on a spot of earth. Totalitarian States do not need "strong selves," but strong bodies standing firmly on a spot of earth. Everything which enervates man's physical existence must be excluded from the arts. In the important English poets we do not find this conception. There is only one and rather strange exception—Collins.

Yet Collins did not warn the "Britons" against "degenerate," enervating and demoralizing art, because he was a worshipper of the State, but for quite personal and most moving reasons: he was pursued by madness, he was sinking into darkness, and he was struggling to cling to sanity and reality:

> Britons! away with the degenerate pack!
> Discard soft nonsense in a slavish tongue,
> The strain insipid and the thought unknown;
> From truth and nature form the unerring test;
> Be what is manly, chaste, and good the best!
> O Britons!
> No longer let unmeaning sounds invite
> To visionary scenes of false delight . . .
> The temper of our isle, though cold, is clear;
> And such our genius, noble though severe.

These lines are not among Collins's best poetry. If he is a poet who still moves us, it is because he sometimes invites us to "visionary scenes of false delight" with more or less "unmeaning sounds." If he still appeals to us, it is because of the suggestive music of lines such as these:

> Alone, if night
> Her travel'd limbs in broken slumbers steep,
> With drooping willows drest, his mournful sprite
> Shall visit sad, perhaps, her silent sleep.

These lines are a typical example of what one could call "dissolving," weakening poetry. They make us forget that we have a solid, tangible body, they make us give up our "strong identity," our "real self," and change us into a soft, melancholy breeze whispering in the night.

The first great English poet whose verse has a dissolving quality is Spenser. When we read him we cannot pay much attention to what he says. His words have the fate of a name written on the sand:

> One day I wrote her name upon the strand,
> But came the waves and washed it away.

It is useless to try to grasp the meaning of Spenser's sentences. Everything he says is always washed away by new waves of sounds and images. His most characteristic poems have neither real beginning nor real end. They run softly and endlessly like "sweet Themmes." His versification, as Hazlitt said, "is the perfection of melting harmony dissolving the soul in pleasure."

This trend of English poetry to melt the soul in a stream of intoxicating sounds whose meaning is of no importance found its supreme expression in Swinburne. In Swinburne all meanings find their end. His poetry is a river flowing in the middle of nothingness, yet those who let themselves be carried away by it are taken to a land, not of terror, but of indifference and oblivion:

> Outside of all the worlds and ages,
> There where the fool is as the sage is,
>   There where the slayer is clean of blood.
> No end, passage, no beginning,
> There where the sinner leaves off sinning,
>   There where the good man is not good.

The magic of Swinburne's poetry changes us into nothing.

Those who have been changed into nothing cannot face nothingness, since they are nothing. Only those who have retained their own reality can be confronted with nothingness.

The terror in front of nothingness makes man become really himself. This terror must be spiritual, not only physical, of course. The greatest of all English poets, Shakespeare, makes us become really ourselves by confronting us with the terror of the unknown.

It is the infinite depth of the unknown, called by religious people God, which gives depth to poetry.

Vaughan describes art as the expression of man's longing for home:

> Celestial natures still
> Aspire for home. This Solomon of old
> By flowers and carvings and mysterious skill
> Of wings and cherubims and palms foretold.

But what is this home? Man

> knows he hath a home, but scarce knows where;
> He says it is so far,
> That he hath quite forgot how to go there.

Man's home is the unknown, and the symbols of poetry which express man's conception of his home cannot be deciphered by reason.

> Here, musing long, I heard
> A rushing wind,
> Which still increased, but whence it stirred,
> Nowhere I could find,

we read in Vaughan. Yet Vaughan as a poet was not great enough to present this "nowhere," the unknown from which we all come, towards which we go, and in which the meaning of our existence lies, so vividly as to frighten us. Shakespeare is so great a poet because his work makes us aware of nothingness in the most disturbing way.

Shakespeare is not a didactic poet; he has nothing to teach us in words directly; yet he makes us become real by compelling us to face the unknown in all its horror. As long as we think we know what reality is, we are unreal. It is only when we dare to face unreality, nothingness, that we become real.

> To sue to live, I find I seek to die,
> And seeking death, find life,

says Claudio.

One of Shakespeare's most important plays is *Troilus and Cressida*. In this work the poet was obsessed with man's "identity," with man's "real self." The characters throughout the play keep making remarks and asking questions such as these: "I say Troilus is Troilus"; "He is himself—Himself! Alas, poor Troilus, I would he were"; "What Cressida is, what Pander, and what we?" These seemingly absurd remarks and questions take a most disturbing significance when one associates them with the words Troilus cries when he discovers Cressida's unfaithfulness: "This is, and is not, Cressid."

Shakespeare makes us become ourselves by showing us the terrifying truth that we cannot be certain of our own identity, that we can be and not be ourselves.

Loyal, manly Hector, the only character in *Troilus and Cressida* who is really and unquestionably himself, falls in the battle. The scene in which Troilus announces Hector's death to the Trojans is one of the most moving pages in Shakespeare. The only one who is really himself and something to hold on to in life is killed, man's reality becomes questionable, and the world an endless void.

> TROILUS. Hector is slain.
> ALL. Hector! the gods forbid!
> TROILUS. He's dead . . .
> ÆNEAS. My lord, you do discomfort all the host.
> TROILUS. You understand me not that tell me so.
> I do not speak of flight, of fear, of death;
> But dare all imminence that gods and men
> Address their dangers in. Hector is gone . . .
> There is a word will Priam turn to stone,
> Make wells and Niobes of maids and wives,
> Cold statues of the youth; and in a word
> Scare Troy out of itself. But march away:
> Hector is dead; there is no more to say.

In Shakespeare's poetry we find the word after which there is nothing more to say. Yet when man finds himself in the middle of the silence and darkness, in which there is nothing more to say, the beginning of a new, more real life becomes possible for him.

This truth has been expressed by another great English poet, Donne, who, like Shakespeare, makes us face nothingness:

> I am re-begot
> Of absence, darkness, death; things which are not.

Keats also knew this truth:

> Aye, on the shores of darkness there is light,
>   And precipices show untrodden green;
> There is a budding morrow in midnight;
>   There is a triple sight in blindness keen.

Yet in Keats's poetry darkness, precipices and death are not real but imaginary ones. Many people who do not think of death as a reality threatening their very existence like to imagine themselves dead, and I am afraid that Keats was one of them.

> I have been half in love with easeful death.
> Called him soft names in many a mused rhyme.

Although Keats knew that one should face nothingness in order to become real, he preferred to lose himself in daydreams about "easeful deaths." Perhaps what he called "death in life" has only a sexual meaning. Many poets when they speak of death, mean something quite different. It is interesting to note that we find a poem in Pope inspired by a "death" surprisingly similar to the one Keats was in love with:

> O the pain, the bliss of dying!
> Cease, fond Nature, cease thy strife,
> And let me languish into life!

These lines have neither the intensity nor the dissolving, the intoxicating quality of Keats's poetry. But if Pope is not as intense a poet as Keats, he has the power to keep us on solid ground and in the light of the day, far from Keats's unreal precipices and nights.

Keats was not always intoxicated, lost in an intense unreality. When he was sober he was most penetrating, and said the most profound things about poetry and man's existence. I do not know what I admire most in his work: the power of his intoxicating verse or the insight of his sober moments. Both versions of "Hyperion" are full of such sober moments. The approaching of real death was depriving imaginary "easeful" death of its fascination, and was forcing the poet to face reality. "Illness," he wrote a few months before he died, ". . . has relieved my mind of a load of deceptive thoughts and images, and makes me perceive things in a truer light."

I should like to conclude these notes with a few words about the two most respected English poets of today: T. S. Eliot and Edith Sitwell.

Although T. S. Eliot's poetry is based on the tradition of the English poets who tried to make man real by compelling him to face nothingness, in its latest phase it has become too detached to be disturbing or compelling in any way. Although in Eliot's recent poems there is much "absence, darkness, death," many "things which are not," I do not see what positive life can spring out of them, unless we consider annihilation in complete detachment as something positive.

Edith Sitwell's recent poetry, which is also very much in the English tradition, is differently substantial. If T. S. Eliot's recent work gives the impression of barrenness, Edith Sitwell's latest poems reveal a world of fertility. There is something very tangible and at the same time universal in her verse: the body of a Greek tragic heroine which suddenly becomes Mother Earth:

> And I, who stood in the grave's clothes of my flesh
> Unutterably spotted with the world's woes
> Cry—"I am Fire! See I am the bright gold
> That shines like a flaming fire in the night—the gold-trained planet—
> The laughing heat of the Sun that was born from darkness
> Returning to darkness—I am fecundity, harvest."

In Edith Sitwell's recent poetry there is an unmistakably Greek quality.

NOTES ON SOME CONTEMPORARY WRITERS

Arts are tools . . . —HERMAN MELVILLE.

I

THOSE who mix up things and expect anything new in the arts to look eccentric wonder why *New Writing*, which never publishes anything particularly eccentric, was given its name. Yet it is clear to anyone who looks carefully into its origins that this periodical was founded in order to combat, besides other things, novelty for novelty's sake in the arts. Its founder and editor, in a poem which he wrote two or three years before the first volume of *New Writing* appeared, and in which he expressed a conception of life and literature common among the writers of his generation, saw the "eccentric style of writing" as a symptom of "illness which brings illness." It was in order to fight what they considered as the illness of the times that the young writers of the 'thirties, who had first collaborated in *New Signatures*, in 1936 came together again, with a number of fresh names, in the pages of the new book-periodical. Writing was a most serious matter to them. The "new" they asked from literature was not novelty, but a healthier, more human world. This world did not come as they expected and prophesied, but, at the moment of failure, another world they were not looking for was revealed to them.

Here I would like to sketch a few thoughts suggested by the search, the adventures, the failure and the success of those among the young writers of the 'thirties whose seriousness was so deep that it made them embark upon that perilous and dramatic journey: the philosophic quest.

One of them, Stephen Spender, who often strikes an astonishing depth in speaking about poetry, in one of his last essays described the poet as "pursuing philosophic truth through interpretation of experience." The poet must be driven to writing poetry by philosophical anxiety—the anxiety which asks: "What is the meaning of life? What do I live for? Why do we live, and why must man suffer?" Sometimes these questions lead to abstract speculations, that is to philosophy in the strict sense, while at other times the anxiety behind them finds outlet and expression in artistic creation. And that is what usually happens in England. The most genuine philosophical anxiety of the English is to be found not so much in the works of their philosophers as in the works of their poets, their dramatists and their novelists. There certainly is more philosophical anxiety in Shakespeare than in Bacon, in Donne than in Locke, in Virginia Woolf than in G. E. Moore. I do not know any English philosopher of today who described the subject of all philosophy as vividly as Virginia Woolf did in *To the Lighthouse*: "The old question which traversed the sky of the soul perpetually, the vast, the general question which was apt to particularize itself at such moments as these, when she released faculties that had been on the strain, stood over her, paused over her, darkened over her. What was the meaning of life? That was all. A simple question; one that tended to close in on one with years. The great revelation had never come. The great revelation perhaps never did come. Instead there were little daily miracles, matches struck unexpectedly in the dark; here was one . . . Life stand still here, Mrs. Ramsay said. 'Mrs. Ramsay! Mrs. Ramsay!' she repeated. All was silence."

This seems to me very similar to what Aristotle must have meant when he described the subject of philosophy as the question always asked and never answered. There is no answer. Silence is what surrounds our lives. But we usually do not realize it. We speak so much and so loudly almost all the time that we forget all about the menace hidden in the silence in which our lives move. If we listened to it we would be profoundly disturbed, and no one likes to be disturbed. Yet sometimes we become aware of the silence which is all round us. We call, but no response comes. What can this mean? Who could tell what it does mean? And anxiety—philosophical anxiety—begins. One has to ask the same question over and over again, but no answer is heard, and the more conscious one becomes of the silence, the more anxious one's questions grow.

Very few people know this anxiety, since very few people take life seriously enough to pay any attention to what surrounds it. Even poets and writers, whom one would expect to face life in all its reality, do not always bother about any ultimate questions. That is why it is so exciting and moving when one detects the tremor of philosophical anxiety in the verse of a poet, especially when this poet is a contemporary.

The passion for truth is what makes so interesting the most gifted among the young poets and writers of the 'thirties.

II

"The true poets must be truthful" they had been taught by Wilfred Owen, the poet whose seriousness had appealed so much to theirs, and to whom they listened more than to anyone else. Writing was a way to find truth for them. In one of his earlier poems John Lehmann described what writing meant to him and, in some way, to all the group of poets who collaborated in *New Signatures* first and, later on, in *New Writing*:

> To penetrate that room is my desire,
> The extreme attic of the mind, that lies
> Just beyond that last bend in the corridor.
> Writing I do it. Phrases, poems are keys.
> Loving's another way (but not so sure).
> A fire's in there, I think, there's truth at last
> Deep in a lumber chest. . . .

These lines are one of the most complete expressions of philosophical anxiety that I know. Those whose mind is disturbed by this anxiety cannot be satisfied with the meaning which life seems to have. They are always looking for another, more satisfactory, more profound meaning hidden behind the appearances of the world. For them beyond all rooms open to common experience, there must be an "extreme attic," a truth, in which one could find a greater security and warmth. There must be a certainty somewhere hidden behind all the uncertainties of life, a secret order behind the disorders of the world. But how can one find them? One is kept awake by the anxiety which never stops asking: "What is the meaning of all this? Is there any meaning at all?" But no one knows how to read the cryptogram. Yet in some moments of extreme concentration, in moments of union with the beloved or in moments of artistic creation, for instance, one sometimes feels that somehow the cryptogram is going to yield its secret. The secret is never revealed, of course; but one is given the impression that if one devoted oneself completely to love or to artistic creation one would be nearer to the meaning of life.

The failure to which all philosophical efforts inevitably lead was described by John Lehmann in this same poem, and by

C. Day Lewis in his *Transitional Poem*, which is a typical example of a work born of philosophical anxiety:

> Sometimes I'm near,
> But draughts puff out the matches, and I'm lost.
> Sometimes I'm lucky, find a key to turn,
> Open an inch or two—but always then
> A bell rings, someone calls, or cries of "fire"
> Arrest my hand when nothing's known or seen,
> And running down the stairs again I mourn.
>
> . . . the flash
> That bleakly enlightens a few sour acres leaves but
> A more Egyptian darkness whence it came.

Nevertheless, in spite of all failures, philosophical anxiety, which grows stronger with each failure, does not let one give it up. "Sleep on, you fells and profound dales," we read in this same poem by Day Lewis:

> There is no
> Material wind or rain can insulate
> The mind against its own forked speculation,
> When once that storm sets in.

Once one has experienced the need to find the meaning of one's life, one cannot easily resign oneself to a life without the hope of a meaning. One must try to find it, even if something tells one that one may never find it. Those who feel that love is the way for them to be nearer to the meaning of their lives must love as much and as completely as they can. Those who feel that writing can give them the key to the "extreme attic of the mind" must apply themselves to writing with all the seriousness of their being. Both ways, of course, are dangerous to everyday happiness. Love as well as artistic creation, when they are taken seriously as ways which could lead to the revelation of the meaning of life and not as pleasures which make one forget the anxiety of one's existence, are full of perils. One must be really brave to choose love or writing as one's guides, because they may lead one to the space in which the meaning of our life is hidden—and who can say that this space may not be the land of death? In the works of all writers who wrote driven by philosophical anxiety one often finds the shudder given by the nearness of death. This shudder often runs through the rhythms of the poets I am considering here. I remember some lines by Auden:

Nights come bringing the snow, and the dead howl
Under the headland in their windy dwelling
Because the Adversary put too easy questions
On lonely roads.

I also remember *A Pure Despair*, which in its bare simplicity is
to me one of the most beautiful poems of the 'thirties:

He did not die with loathing for the worms,
Or fear of pain, or tunnel's gloom ahead,
But with a pure despair refusing terms
That suns of summer for their kindness made,
Turned his desire from green and flowered growth
To rocky dark and long before he died,
A lonely miner, worked new ores of death.

III

But to the young writers of the 'thirties writing did not only
mean a way by which they could come nearer to the truth they
needed as individuals. They had grown up in the midst of the
disorder and suffering of the last war and of the years which followed the war, and the problems of disorder and suffering never
stopped haunting them. But in their earlier works it is not only
the feeling that there is something wrong with the world as it is
which strikes me. These young writers were conscious of something else too—of their own lives as full of possibilities, promises
and aspirations. And the strength and hope of youth that was in
them made them feel that they had a mission to fulfil. The world
was not as it should be; it needed changing; and since they felt
strong and full of life, why not do all they could for this changing? Poetry is a power. Why waste it, and not use it for putting
right the things that were wrong? Poetry should be used for
creating history.

The young writers of the 'thirties looked at the "truly great"
of history with jealous eyes. They wanted to become makers of
history themselves, creators of a new man and a new society in
which there would be no disorder and no suffering. "Writing"
could help not only their own selves, but also others to find the
meaning of life. Their ambition as writers was boundless: they
wanted to abolish human misery.

Only people who know nothing of the poetry of the 'thirties
can describe it simply as "Marxist" or "Freudian." What obsessed

its poets primarily was human misery, not as it was described by
Marx or Freud, but as they came to know it themselves, and the
new society and the new man they were prophesying were not
simply second-hand visions of Marx or Freud, but above all
creations of their own poetic imaginations. They wanted a social
revolution, because there was too much disorder and suffering in
society as it was. They also wanted man free from inhibitions and
denials, which mean illness, unhappiness and deadening of life.
They dreamed of a society based on the love of man for man, and
of a man who would be a man. There is a well-known poem by
Stephen Spender—*Oh young men, oh young comrades*—in which
the coming free men, free from the bonds of society and from
those of their own selves, are invoked:

> Oh comrades, step beautifully from the solid wall
> Advance to rebuild and sleep with friend on hill
> Advance to rebel and remember what you have
> No ghost ever had, immured in his hall.

Such dreams of a beautiful, luminous and joyful humanity were
only one of the ways by which the preoccupation of the poets with
the ugliness, greyness and misery oppressing and deadening man
was expressed. In some of their prose works—for instance, John
Lehmann's *Evil was Abroad*—one can see what the suffering
caused by social injustice meant to the writers of the 'thirties. It
was a kind of cipher of the meaning of life to them. Their sympathy for the poor and the oppressed sprang out of their need to
approach man in all his reality, out of their fear to be excluded
from a most significant part of life. The desire to make out the
meaning of a humanity oppressed and deformed physically and
mentally by social injustice became to the writer of the 'thirties a
craving "like the need for light, or water." The hero of *Evil was
Abroad* felt that the close contact with the oppressed "was bringing him new understanding of the poetry" in which he was
interested, "just as much as the poetry was bringing him towards
the living." In this remark I find much that explains the passionate interest of the poets of the 'thirties in social problems. It was
their philosophical anxiety, the anxiety that made them write in
order to penetrate deeper into truth, which also made them
attempt to enter the lives of the starving, to meet them in sympathy and friendship with no social barriers between them as
human beings.

I'm jealous of the weeping hours
They stare through with such hungry eyes,

wrote Stephen Spender;

I'm haunted by these images,
I'm haunted by their emptiness.

In *The Losers*, one of C. Day Lewis's most disturbing poems, we can clearly see how closely related to their philosophical anxiety was the interest of the poets in social justice:

What can we say of these from the womb wasted,
Whose nerve was never tested in act, who fell at the start,
Who had no beauty to lose, born out of season?

Early an iron frost clamped their flowing
Desires. They were lost at once: they failed and died in the whirling
Snow, bewildered, homeless from first to last.

Frightened we stop our ears to the truth they are telling
Who toil to remain alive, whose children start from sleep
Weeping into a world worse than nightmares.

At the time when *New Writing* was being founded, the poets were obsessed with the truth which the poor and oppressed, "the losers," were telling more than with anything else. The first numbers of the new publication appeared to many as pure revolutionary propaganda. But they were a great deal more than that. They expressed the philosophical anxiety of their young contributors, who felt impelled to fix their eyes upon human misery in order to read its disturbing meaning. What they read in it was more than the necessity of a social revolution. It is interesting to compare the end of *Evil was Abroad* with a poem by David Gascoyne. This is what I read in the novel:

"He was haunted by the description of the dishevelled outskirts of a city at twilight. . . . As he went over it in memory, he found himself making the scene curiously exact: there was a lamp which had just been lit, behind the black back-wall of an unfinished, isolated house-block, and beyond was a sort of common, covered with scrap-iron and rubbish. And then, just as if he were watching a film or play, he saw a figure cross the common, with head averted; and the figure was unmistakably Rudi, from the hair, from the way he moved. . . ."

And here are a few lines from the poem which this passage brought into my mind:

> And in a flash
> Of insight I behold the field's
> Apotheosis: No man's land
> Between this world and the beyond,
> Remote from men and yet more real
> ° Than any human dwelling place:
> A tabernacle where one stands
> As though within the empty space
> Round which revolves the Sage's Wheel.

IV

What is interesting in the early volumes of *New Writing* is not propaganda, but the expression of the philosophical anxiety of its contributors, who, craving for truth and justice, had to stop and concentrate before the most baffling cipher, the fact of injustice and suffering. Stephen Spender, who wrote:

> There is no consolation, no, none
> In the curving beauty of that line
> Traced on our graphs through history, where the oppressor
> Starves and deprives the poor.
>
> Paint here no draped despairs, no saddening clouds
> Where the soul rests, proclaims eternity.
> But let the wrong cry out as raw as wounds
> This Time forgets and never heals, far less transcends;

Stephen Spender said in one of his latest essays—actually in the same essay in which he described the poet as "pursuing philosophic truth": "It is as well to keep this suffering of humanity in the forefront of our picture of the situation of the poet-artist. It is far truer to do so than to talk of the Pink Decade, Left Wing, and so on, terms which tend to be fashionable jargon." If one thinks that the preoccupation of the young writers of the 'thirties with human suffering was more important than their "communism," one will find that these writers have not changed much since their revolutionary days. Even if they have stopped writing as if they were making communist propaganda, they have never stopped being revolutionary. Now they must hate the order of the world as it is even more than they used to before. Today the meaning of human suffering must appear to them more baffling, more disturbing than a few years ago. Their own bewilderment has gone even deeper and has become a terrifying knowledge.

It seems as if the poetry of the 'thirties has been a failure. The change which it preached and prophesied has not come; the evils which it tried to prevent have not been prevented; the dream of a new humanity has proved only a dream. Its words seem as if they dissolved in nothing. Even the poets themselves know that they failed.

But failure is something spiritually fruitful. Those who wrote because they wanted to know more about truth, the meaning of life, the reality of man, have been taught much by their failure. Failure reveals the terrifying abyss over which humanity moves, better than anything else. And it is this abyss which gives depth to human existence. In the works of these poets man has now taken his proper depth, at least in the works of those among them who have not been led to aberrations, because some of the young writers of the 'thirties have been led into aberrations.

Sometimes a man haunted by philosophical anxiety loses patience and begins to think that a seemingly quicker and easier way to truth is preferable to the long and difficult one. One such seemingly quicker and easier way is mysticism, another is intellectualism.

The first seems to have been taken recently by Christopher Isherwood, the most talented, perhaps, of all the young prose writers of the 'thirties. Mysticism is a way of life which from time to time gives one the experience of personal annihilation in the depths of a night in which there are no distinctions, no differences, no divisions, no conflicts, in which all is one, and in which one is not separate from all. This is achieved by a negation of the intellect, this power which struggles to keep one in a lighted and divided world. To get rid of the intellect and sink oneself into the depths of a night, which seems the only reality, is, to my mind, a much too easy and much too doubtful way to truth.

Auden in his *New Year Letter* seems to have taken the opposite, but equally doubtful way to truth, intellectualism. Intellect has always been a danger in Auden's poetry, but in his best moments its mobile and cold unreality was always filled with the glowing and solid reality of feeling. His intellect did dance even then, but its dance was not empty, but full of a warm and suffering reality. Personally I prefer those lines of his which move in a slow way, in which there is more solidity of feeling than agility of intellect, such as:

> Doom is dark and deeper than any sea-dingle.
> Upon what man it fall
> In spring, day-wishing flowers appearing,
> Avalanche sliding, white snow from rock-face,
> That he should leave his house,
> No cloud-soft hand can hold him, restraint by women;
> But ever that man goes
> Through place-keepers, through forest trees,
> A stranger to strangers over undried sea,
> Houses for fishes, suffocating water,
> Or lonely on fell as chat,
> By pot-holed becks
> A bird stone-haunting, an unquiet bird.

Unfortunately, in *New Year Letter* he let his intellect dance free from much passion, and when the intellect comes and goes left to itself, or almost to itself, its dance is empty of real meaning, graceless, boring and useless. It does not lead anywhere. It plays with all the words philosophers use as tools for finding truth in abstract speculations, but the play is only a play, it does not make much sense. It is painful to make this remark about a poet whom I had much in mind when at the beginning of this essay I wrote about the seriousness of the young writers of the 'thirties.

V

Both these writers, Isherwood and Auden, expatriated themselves from England a little while before the war broke out. Those who remained at home—and I do not want to say by this that home is the best place for the quest of truth—remained also in the difficult and necessary way they had to follow. They accepted their failure with humility and dignity. Even Cecil Day Lewis, the proudest of all poets of his generation, who until quite recently preferred to keep out of his verse anything that could sound like the confession of defeat, or even of weakness, as if it were not becoming to a man to feel his weakness, or be defeated —even proud Day Lewis confessed his failure and his grief in a most moving, but not less masculine or poetic way than when he sung his power and triumphs:

> It is the logic of our times,
> No subject for immortal verse,
> That we who lived by honest dreams,
> Defend the bad against the worse.

Such an acceptance of the duty imposed by reality on the dreamer is the best proof that his dreams were really honest. It is moving to remember what illusions about the power of verse the poet used to have, while one reads this:

> Our words like poppies love the maturing field
> But form no harvest:
> May lighten the innocent's pang, or paint the dreams
> Where guilt is unharnessed.
> Dark over all, absolving all, is hung
> Death's vaulted patience:
> Words are to set man's joy and suffering there
> In constellations.

Humanity which has always been in the centre of C. Day Lewis's poetry, as in the works of all the most gifted writers of his generation, is now pictured in his work, as in theirs, more complete, deeper, as if with one more dimension, the metaphysical one:

> Always our time's ghost-guise of impermanence
> Daunts me; whoever I meet,
> Wherever I stand, a shade of parting lengthens
> And laps around my feet.
> But now, the heart-sunderings, the real migrations—
> Millions fated to flock
> Down weeping roads to mere oblivion—strike me
> Dumb as a rooted rock.

Here humanity is represented in the dark infinite which surrounds it and which belongs to it. The poets who were trying to embrace the complete man in their works have now discovered his metaphysical depth. For them now Man is more than a mere physical, psychological and social reality; he is also a metaphysical one. And that makes him infinite. Infinite as his solitude, or eternity.

This new image of man is now to be found not only in Cecil Day Lewis's poems, but also in Stephen Spender's recent poems— in the end of *The Ambitious Son*, in *Fates*, and in the all-embracing *Elegy*—and with a disturbing and powerful suggestiveness in John Lehmann's last poems. In his prose poems *Vigils,* the person addressed is seen "out there, in that black, heaving desert of the sea," or "among the white skulls and sandstorms of Africa," in the terrifying emptiness surrounding man's life. This empty space and the greatness of man in it, of man who fills the boundless void with the boundlessness of his solitude and despair, are suggested with the most haunting power in *Summer Story*. Here are the last lines of the poem:

> . . . Those comrades from the citadel
>
> One afternoon of dust and songs
> Turned, and were swallowed in the glare; .
> Yet still goodbye, though few remained
> Grew like a weed of rank despair,
>
> Till I was left alone to meet
> (As I had always known must be)
> In the damp house, at summer's end,
> The dark Lieutenant from the sea.

The poetry of the 'thirties has not been in vain, since it led to this new land, which, although it is not the country this poetry was dreaming of, is a space in which man is seen in all his greatness. No one thinks that Colombus failed because, instead of discovering the route to Cathay, he discovered America. The poets we have considered here started their voyage dreaming of a new man. They did not find this man in flesh, but, instead of him, when one night they stranded upon the rock of necessity, an image of man that exceeded in greatness all they had ever dared to dream of was revealed to them. Their failure was their success.

CHARLOTTE BRONTË

It is a little difficult to take Charlotte Brontë seriously at first. When I read her best-known novel, *Jane Eyre,* although the book enthralled me and I could not leave it until I had finished it, I found myself thinking at every page, even every sentence: "This is a book written by a governess for other governesses." Indeed, all the feelings and thoughts which spring from an inferiority complex in a governess, all her envy and hate against her employers, all the wishful fantasies which make her existence possible, are described in this book without the slightest restraint. All the society women are shown as incredibly common and vulgar; all the governesses are perfect examples of ladies.

When, in the works of Charlotte Brontë, one comes across characters whose social position one has not yet been told and who are described as "ladies in every point," "all delicacy and cultivation," one can be certain that in the next few pages they will be shown to be governesses in sentences like these: "Each held a situation in families by whose wealthy and haughty members they were regarded only as humble dependants and who neither knew nor sought out their innate excellencies, and appreciated only their acquired accomplishments as they appreciated the skill of their cook or the taste of their waiting woman." Can one help smiling at such sentences? Can one argue with those who have described the author as one of those governesses who expect their mistress to be more interested in their personal feelings than in their children's new teeth? Even if one wanted to defend the writer by trying to show that she was not at all that kind of person, she herself would prove one wrong with numerous sentences such as I have quoted above.

Charlotte Brontë, who had no sense of humour and no sense of proportion when it was a question of her personal affairs and misfortunes, wrote many pages on these full of a passion and a pain which are exceedingly amusing. But passion and pain when they are genuine, even though we may find them amusing, force us in the end to take them seriously. And this explains the place which, in spite of her great faults, Charlotte Brontë holds and will always hold in the history of the human mind.

Her works, although written in this oddly uncertain taste, fascinate us with the intensity of her pain, which even when it takes the form of envy and unsatisfied sexual hunger makes us laugh, but at the same time feel the deepest sympathy with her. I say "with her" and not "with her characters" because all the characters in her books were merely means through which she interpreted her own pain. When one reads Jane Austen's *Emma* one is mainly interested in the adventures of the principal character of the book, whereas when one reads *Jane Eyre* or *Villette* one is not so much interested in the adventures of the principal characters as in the misfortunes of the writer which these adventures reveal to us.

To this is also due, to a large extent, the exceptional interest in Charlotte Brontë's life. Shortly after her death one of her friends, Mrs. Gaskell, published *The Life of Charlotte Brontë,* which is considered one of the best works of English biography. This book, however, in spite of its many qualities—the conscientiousness, sympathy, warmth which make it so lively—is limited by the omissions made necessary by the austere standards of the time, and therefore ignores or even misinterprets Charlotte Brontë's misfortunes, which, as her novels show, had the most important bearing on her life. The discovery of new sources, as well as the research carried out as a result of the great interest aroused by these misfortunes, have filled the gaps in Mrs. Gaskell's Victorian biography. And even when the sources are silent the writer herself has said so much that we are left in no doubt. There is perhaps no other writer in English literature about whose private misfortunes and most intimate personality we know so much.

Charlotte Brontë, who was herself so odd, belonged to a very odd family. Her years of childhood were spent on the Yorkshire moors, well known for their wild solitude, in a home built of grey stone next to a graveyard and perhaps on old graves. She had lost her mother, and lived with a strange, bad-tempered father who was the village parson, and with her five young sisters and brother who, like herself, had nothing childlike about them, but were as serious and wise as old men.

Many years later, when all his children were dead, Father Brontë told with pride a story which today makes us shudder at the grey solemnity of Charlotte's childhood. "When my chil-

dren were very young, when, as far as I can remember, the
eldest was about ten years of age, and the youngest about four,
thinking that they knew more than I had yet discovered, in
order to make them speak with less timidity, I deemed that if
they were put under a sort of cover I might gain my end; and
happening to have a mask in the house, I told them all to stand
and speak boldly from under cover of the mask.

"I began with the youngest (Anne, afterwards Acton Bell) and
asked what a child like her most wanted; she answered 'Age and
experience.' I asked the next (Emily, afterwards Ellis Bell) what
I had best do with her brother Branwell, who was sometimes a
naughty boy; she answered, 'Reason with him, and when he
won't listen to reason, whip him.' I asked Branwell what was the
best way of knowing the difference between the intellects of man
and woman; he answered, 'By considering the difference between
them as to their bodies.' I then asked Charlotte what was the best
book in the world; she answered, 'The Bible.' And what was the
next best; she answered, 'The Book of Nature.' I then asked the
next what was the best mode of education for a woman; she
answered, 'That which would make her rule her house well.'
Last, I asked the oldest what was the best mode of spending time;
she answered, 'By laying it out in preparation for a happy
eternity.' "

These answers, which to us today would sound monstrously
precocious and unnatural, even on the lips of young people approaching maturity, show how utterly serious and unchildlike
had been the upbringing of the Brontës, set in the windswept
wilderness of the moors, in the unploughed land of the wild
flowers of the heath—flowers that have neither gay colour nor
vital sap. When Charlotte was eight her father sent her, together
with her two elder sisters, to a charity school for the daughters
of parsons, that was greyer, poorer and even less humane than
their graveyard home. There Charlotte experienced hunger,
breathed the infected air of disease, and came to know death
at close quarters. Death, which had always coloured the young
Brontës' thoughts, as we have seen by their answers to their
father, revealed itself to Charlotte in all its fearful nakedness
when it took away her two elder sisters. And the nine-year-old
child felt the chaos of nothingness which gapes before us and
in which we are in danger of falling any moment. "My mind,"

she wrote later in her memoirs of the school, which are, in fact, one of the most impressive parts of her work, ". . . felt the one point where it stood—the present; all the rest was formless cloud and vacant depth; and it shuddered at the thought of tottering, and plunging amid that chaos." And this was not the only serious revelation which she experienced at the orphanage. She realized there that she was ugly. One day a little schoolfellow of hers, with whom she became friends for the rest of her life, told her so, and this new realization, though of no metaphysical importance, became of greater significance in her life and work than the sense of chaos and nothingness that shook her for a moment. Charlotte had very little metaphysical spirit, and she was never able to understand the mystic life of her sister Emily. Though we cannot say that she was entirely absorbed by the physical world, yet her inner life was only a craving for what, as she would say, fate had denied her: health, beauty, love and fulfilment—gifts which a metaphysical and mystic spirit or a religious one would have considered superficial. But we are certain that, had she been able to change what she called her "inner wealth" for more physical gifts, she would have done it gladly. For she was possessed by a thirst for life and especially for love. Yet very early, from her schooldays, she knew that she had none of the gifts which could make such a life possible for her. Both her portrait by her brother Branwell, painted when she was very young, and Richmond's, painted very much later, apparently flatter her so much that we cannot realize from them the ugliness that made her suffer so deeply. Towards the end of her life, a short time before her wedding, she confessed to a friend of hers, who later wrote her biography, that she noticed that her guests, having looked at her once, averted their eyes from the part of the room where she herself remained. This persistent obsession about her unpleasant looks made her see people— men and women, but especially women—in a certain way; an ugly woman's way. Her work is a curious and unique document of what and how such a person can see. First, feminine beauty did not seem to her a natural gift, but an anomaly, an injustice and a crime of heaven against her. All her heroines were ugly, and even when she decided to make the two leading women in *Shirley* beautiful, it is important to notice that the time comes when the beauty is made to wither; she does not just say that his or that woman was beautiful, but says, "To her had not been denied the gift of beauty." And this admission is an exception in her work which usually declares the rights and charms of ugliness. Whenever she introduces beautiful women her purpose is to show the emptiness and inner ugliness hidden by beauty. And as we must expect the governesses, whenever they appear, to represnt good breeding, while the ladies show their inferior "governess" quality; so we must expect the immense insignificance and unworthiness of the beautiful women soon to be shown up—while with the ugly there is always an eventual disclosure of their deep inner beauty.

Naturally in this there is the personal sensitiveness of the authoress and an almost shameless advertising of her charms. And I have already said that George Richmond's portrait is not a criterion of her looks.

The amusing thing is when she imagines a man's taste in women, her portrait is always his ideal. Listen, for example, to the words of one of her heroes. "I am no Oriental," is the typical opening, and in this she condemns all men who have the bad taste to admire physical attraction. "I am no Oriental. White necks, carmine lips and cheeks, clusters of bright curls, do not suffice for me without that Promethean spark which will live after the roses and lilies are faded, the burnished hair grown grey. In sunshine, in prosperity, the flowers are very well; but how many days are there in life—November seasons of disaster, when a man's hearth and home would be cold indeed without the clear cheering gleam of intellect." Charlotte saw her personal charms as such a "clear cheering gleam" hidden in an unattractive body, "the smallest I ever saw," and in a young face deprived of youth, and she felt that to be admired and charming she only needed a loving eye to look at her. "A loving eye is all the charm needed: to such you are handsome enough; or rather your sternness has a power beyond beauty. . . ."

But did she ever find such an eye? We cannot say no, because the Rev. A. B. Nichols, who married her near the end of her life, when she was faded and almost gone, saw behind her ugliness a charm which made him depend entirely on her for his happiness. Unfortunately, Charlotte did not want this kind of love. She was not attracted by Mr. Nichols—at least, before their marriage—for he was not her type, and those whom she loved never looked at her with loving eyes. As her friend Miss Martineau, an intellectual and author of philosophical works, remarked in her criticism of *Villette*, wounding Charlotte's sensitiveness so much that she broke her friendship with her for ever, "All the female characters, in all their thoughts and lives, are full of one thing, or are regarded by the reader in the light of that one thought—love . . . events and characters are to be regarded through the medium of one passion only." This comment would not be considered unfavourable criticism today, since the most significant novel of our times, the great work of Proust, is nothing but a long and detailed proof of the truth that love is never requited. But Charlotte was deeply wounded by her friend's remark, because it made her more conscious of the great suffering and failure of her life, whose most vital need was the love that she never found.

But let us now examine the facts.

We have left Charlotte a young girl at school. Her first unrequited love happened also at a school, but many years later—after seventeen years. Between these two stages of her life there was a long and joyless period of family cares interrupted by a few years of school life, either as a student or a teacher, and two bitter attempts to make her living as a governess. We have already mentioned the last period of her life, which produced some of her most amusingly bitter pages. Let us now make haste to consider the greatest love of her life.

At about the end of 1841, bored with her life, which did not satisfy her great thirst for full living and was not at all life with a capital L, she decided to try to go to Belgium on the pretext of perfecting her French, but really with the deeper and perhaps unconscious purpose of *living*. An aunt of hers who was staying with them was persuaded to lend the necessary money, and so at the beginning of 1842, when she was twenty-six and had already started to show premature and interesting signs of age, she left her home with her sister Emily to go to Heger's in Brussels, which has since become famous for its associations with them. This long building in the Rue d'Isabel with the great back gardens and the *allée défendue* does not now exist except in Charlotte's work, where it is described accurately and in detail. How could this scene in which the great tragedy of her life was set not have left an impression of horror on her? The school was run by M. Heger and his wife, apparently very human creatures, though in Charlotte's work they appear as satanical beings with supernatural powers both for good and evil. Of course, this is not unnatural, for she saw M. Heger as a lover, while Madame Heger was to her the wicked spirit that stood between her and her beloved. He was a short, lean, agile, dark man—a dogmatic, dictatorial and impatient teacher who loved to teach and behaved in social life as if he were in a class-room with his pupils. Charlotte, of course, was a good student, took her work seriously, was intelligent about his lectures and wrote good essays. It was natural for him to single her out and show interest in her. Charlotte interpreted his interest as love, and was deeply disturbed by what she took to be a sexual approach. Her ugliness made her feel desperate, and many times she hesitated to look at him, afraid that he might avoid her glance. Yet he did not seem to find her repulsive. Often she let her eyes rest on him, and he did not avoid them like the others. He—"her teacher"—how that "he" moved her. It made him her own almost as much as an embrace. He, who was so intellectual, could not be "an Oriental" in his taste, and of course her physical ugliness could not worry him. On the contrary, her intelligent face would be beautiful to him and he must enjoy looking at her. What an important part glances had in this silent drama! It was not only her own that were full of "modesty and expression," as she imagined; it was not only his which were for her a subject for endless study, but there were also those of the other students who had youth and charm that made her despair of her own ugliness. Full of suspicion, she followed their every movement and glance, and everywhere she saw nothing but the most vulgar and unmentionable designs. She never missed an opportunity later of attacking these "vicious and repulsive" *Lesbascouriennes*, as she called them, and she finally spoke more freely about them and revenged herself in *Villette*. In her novel *The Professor* she describes the glances that tortured her as if in a nightmare; "languishing, provoking, leering, laughing." It was not only these. There were also sounds that were full of meaning: "sometimes she sighs, sometimes groans, sometimes utters inarticulate sounds," things for which she had no words, and, worst of all, "she put out her foot that it may touch mine." The thing that comforted her was that "we scorn what, unasked, is lavishly offered." And she·was trying to fight all these external enemies with her inner weapons; with her restrained expression and, above all, with her essays. Each of them had as much value as all the suggestive glances of her rivals put together. (They were suggestive, too, in their over-dressing to attract attention.) Her essays were one long and desperate cry for love. She wrote of Napoleon and she meant the man she loved, his hardness and her passion for him. This essay contains all the nuances of a Theocritean idyll hidden under school phrases which at first glance mean something entirely different. This tragic love, naturally, was not so intense at the beginning, and there was also a respite. After an eight months' stay at the Belgian College the two sisters had to return hastily to England because their aunt was seriously ill. She had died by the time they got back, and Charlotte stayed at home wondering whether she should go back to the dangerous college. But a warm letter from M. Heger to her father, full of interest which might have been taken for sexual interest by a woman in love, made her decide to return and, as she wrote later to a friend, without any explanation for her decision: "I returned to Brussels after Aunt's death against my conscience, prompted by what seemed then an irresistible impulse. I was punished for my selfish folly by a total hindrance for more than two years of happiness and peace of mind."

This kind of story could not end happily. Yet it had its peculiar delight, a tragic delight, "a pleasure like what the thirst-perishing man might feel who knows the well to which he has crept is poisoned, yet stoops and drinks divine draughts nevertheless." It is unnecessary to go on with the sad story, which resulted in Charlotte having to return to England and leave the school and Belgium at the end of the year. In the meantime she had ceased to be a student and taught English at the College. Her new position did not bring her into contact with "her teacher" as much as before, but the worst was that Madame Heger, having realized the English girl's passion for her hus-band, tried to check it, at first by avoiding any emotional scenes, and finally, very skilfully, by making Charlotte leave the school. It is said that Charlotte threatened her before she went away that she was going to have her revenge. And she took this revenge with her pen, as she did with her young school rivals—not only when she drew her as one of the main characters in her novels, as Mlle. Reuter in *The Professor* and as Madame Beck in *Villette,* but also even in works like *Shirley,* where there was no room for such a character as Madame Heger, when Charlotte interrupted the narrative and spoke as Charlotte Brontë herself about the woman she hated: "I remember once seeing a pair of blue eyes, that were usually thought sleepy, secretly on the alert, and I knew by their expression, which chilled my blood—it was in that quarter so wondrously unexpected—that for years they had been accustomed to silent soul-reading. The world called the owner of those blue eyes 'Bonne petite femme' (she was not an Englishwoman): I learned her nature afterwards— got it off by heart—studied it in its farthest, most hidden recesses —she was the finest, subtlest schemer in Europe." Feelings of hatred and more violent feelings of love tortured Charlotte Brontë when she returned home. Her sole consolation was her correspondence with her beloved, though she never dared to use that name, and though his answers were very rare at the beginning and later hardly came at all, yet Charlotte, sacrificing her pride, which was so precious to her, continued to send him the outpourings of her love in letters which were no longer school essays, but true confessions of love. Four of these have been preserved in a most miraculous way; they were torn twice and thrown away; they were recovered, put together, carefully kept, and finally were presented by M. Heger's son to the British Museum. And so we have today the most moving letters that un- requited love could inspire:

"Dîtes-moi enfin ce que vous voulez mon maître mais dîtes moi quelque chose. Ecrire à une ci-devant sous-maîtresse (non— je ne veux pas me souvenir de mon emploi de sous-maîtresse je le renie) mais enfin, écrire à une ancienne élève ne peut-être une occupation fort intéressante pour vous—je le sais—mais pour moi c'est la vie. Votre dernière lettre m'a servi de soutiens—de nourriture pendant six mois—à present il m'en faut un autre et vous me le donnerez—pas parceque vous avez pour moi de l'amitié—vous ne pouvez en avoir beaucoup—mais parceque vous avez l'âme compatissante et que vous ne condamnierez per- sonne à de longues souffrances pour vous épargner quelques momentsd'ennui. Me défendre à vous écrire, refuser de me répon- dre ce sera de m'arracher la seule joie que j'ai au monde, me priver de mon dernier privilège—privilège auquel je ne consentirai jamais a renoncer volontairement. Croyez-moi, mon maître, en écrivant vous faites un bon œuvre—tant que vous crois assez content de moi, tant que j'ai l'espoir de recevoir de vos nouvelles je puis être tranquille et pas trop triste mais quand un silence morne et prolonge semble m'avertir de l'éloignement de mon maître à mon égard—quand de jour en jour j'attends une lettre et que de jour en jour le désappointement vient me rejeter dans un douloureux accablement et que cette douce joie de voir votre écriture, de lire vos conseils me fuit comme une vaine vision, alors, j'ai la fièvre—je perds l'appétit et le sommeil—je dépéris.

"Que ne puis-je avoir pour vous juste autant d'amitié que vous avez pour moi—ni plus ni moins? Je serais alors si tranquille si libre—je pourrais garder le silence pendant six ans sans effort."

When she wrote that his letter has sustained her "pendant six mois," it was no figure of speech. M. Heger had, in fact, asked her to write to him only once in every six months. And Charlotte had made a superhuman effort to comply with his wish. But M. Heger did not answer even then. Charlotte thought that Madame Heger had interfered and stopped her letters from reaching him, and she tried to find a safe way of communicating with him. The way was found. The father of one of her friends was going to Brussels, and she made him promise to see M. Heger and give him her letter. But when he returned from Belgium, though he had fulfilled his mission, he brought her no answer either by word or letter. "Ayant bien compris ces mots," was the last cry of the loving woman, "je me suis dit, ce que je dirais a une autre en pareille circonstances. 'Il faut vous résigner et, surtout ne pas vous affliger d'un malheur que vous n'avez pas mérité.' Je me suis efforcée à ne pas pleurer à ne pas me plaindre——

"Mais quand on ne se plaint pas et qu'on vent se dominer en tyran—les facultés se revoltent—et on paie le calme extérieur par une lutte intérieure presque insupportable.

"Jour et nuit je ne trouve ni repos ni paix—si je dors je fais des rêves tourmentants où je vous voir toujours sévère, toujours sombre et irrité contre moi——

"Pardonnez-moi donc Monsieur si je prends la partie de vous écrire encore—Comment puis-je supporter la vie si je ne fais pas un effort pour en alléger les souffrances?

"Je sais que vous serez impatienté quand vous lirez cette lettre
—Vous direz encore que je suis exaltée—que j'ai des pensées
noires, etc. Soit Monsieur—je ne cherche pas à me justifier, je
me soumets à toutes sortes de reproches—tout ce que je sais—
c'est que je ne puis pas—que je ne veux pas me résigner à perdre
entièrement l'amitié de mon maître—j'aime mieux subir les plus
grands douleurs physiques que d'avoir toujours le cœur lacéré
par des regrets cuisants. Si mon maître me retire entièrement
son amitié je serai tout a fait sans espoir—s'il en donne un peu—
très peu—je serai contente—heureuse, j'aurai un motif pour
vivre—pour travailler.

"Monsieur, les pauvres n'ont pas besoin de grand'chose pour
vivre—ils ne demandent que les miettes de pain qui tombe de
la table des riches—mais si on les refuse les miettes de pain—ils
meurent de faim—Moi non plus je n'ai pas besoin de beaucoup
d'affection de la part de ceux que j'aime je ne saurais que faire
d'une amitié entière et complète—je n'y suis pas habituée—mais
vous me témoigniez autrefois, *un peu* d'intérêt, quand j'étais
votre élève à Bruxelles—et je tiens à conserver ce *peu* d'intérêt—
j'y tiens comme je tiendrais à la vie.

"Vous me direz peutêtre—Je ne vous porte plus le moindre
intérêt Mademoiselle Charlotte—vous n'êtes plus de ma Maison
—je vous ai oubliée.

"Eh bien Monsieur dites moi cela franchement—ce sera pour
moi un choc—n'importe ce sera toujours moins hideux que
l'incertitude.

"Je ne veux pas relire cette lettre—je l'envoie comme je l'ai
écrite—Pourtant j'ai comme la conscience obscure qu'il y a des
personnes froides et sensées qui diraient en la lisant—'elle
déraisonne'—Pour toute vengeance—je souhaite à ces personnes
—un seul jour des tourments que j'ai subis depuis huit mois—on
verrait alors si elles (ne) déraisonneraient pas de même."

But she received no answer even to this letter, and perhaps
there would have been no solution but madness if the solution
of creative work had not appeared. A few days after the desperate
letter that was a last effort for salvation, the three sisters started
to work on the publication of their poems at their own expense.
We shall not concern ourselves with Charlotte's poems, which
were no more than the attempts of a romantic schoolgirl. But
about the same time each of the three sisters started preparing

a novel. So Charlotte found her way of salvation. She found in
her writing love, revenge and everything that life had not given
her. Her first novel, *The Professor*, which was not published till
after her death, was the sad life-story of a teacher who succeeded
in overcoming all the attacks of a devilish headmistress.

*   *   *   *   *

In *Jane Eyre* it was not the superficial characteristics of
Madame Heger that Charlotte drew, but her rival's hidden and
destructive power. In order to express all the terror this power
made her feel, she personified it in a bestial lunatic hidden from
the world's eyes who crept out at night to kill her husband and
tear his bride's wedding veil. In this way Madame Heger's secret
wickedness, usually submerged, broke out just before the fulfilment of Charlotte's happiness and ruined it. But while in reality
the wicked power prevailed over goodness, in the novel it is
finally destroyed by a supernatural justice. And this was to be
expected, for Charlotte Brontë's works were not only an improved version of her past, but also a wish-fulfilment. And these
fantasy love scenes often become tedious in *Jane Eyre*. Rochester's
sweet words and other tendernesses were perhaps necessary to
Charlotte, but to us today they appear crude and in bad taste.
Charlotte also satisfied her cravings in *Shirley*, the first part of
which is a persistent effort to describe the daily habits—we might
almost say the physical habits—of a man. She accompanies him
at his meals, his walks, his chats—even when he bends down to
take off his boots—and tries to identify herself with all his movements by detailed and objective description, as she would have
done had the man been her own husband. But about the middle
of the novel—when she must have realized that this way of possessing a man is only an empty fantasy—she wrote: "The wind,
the cloud's shadow does not pass more silently, more emptily
than he"—yes, then she realized that fantasies have not the
physical solidity that love demands, withdrew again into herself, remembered her sorrows, and started lamenting the injustice that had been done to her in the past and her present
miserable mental and physical condition which deprived her
of hopes for the future. These personal cares made her almost
philosophical, and there are a few passages which we might
regard as expressions of philosophical anxiety if the rest of the

context did not prove it false. ". . . . And what am I—standing here in shadow, shrinking into concealment, my mind darker than my hiding-place? I am one of this world, no spirit, a poor doomed mortal, who asks in ignorance and hopelessness wherefore she was born, to what end she lives; whose mind for ever runs on the question, how she shall at last encounter and by whom be sustained through death?" In these questions it is not a philosophic anxiety, which is always characterized by a certain integrity of purpose and is general, that we find, but the agony of a girl who has very little hope of escaping a spinster's life.

Charlotte's terror at the prospect of becoming an old maid is clearly expressed in *Shirley*. Her changes of mood from the objective to the subjective had a damaging effect on the novel's composition and introduced incoherences into its plot.

But this was not all. During the time she was writing this work Charlotte lost not only her brother Branwell, but also Emily, that unique and extraordinary being who was the model for one of the heroines of the book. This model, which Charlotte adored, although she had not the power to understand her in all her depth, was gone before she had finished her book. We might say that the end of the book was written without enthusiasm or real interest. The figures of the dead brother and sister that haunted the solitude of her home did not leave room for reminiscences or fantasies of love. But ever since the publication of *Jane Eyre* and the resounding success it met with, Charlotte had not belonged exclusively to her home; she was also a public figure. It was then that the second important passion of her life stirred in her: the passion which Mrs. Gaskell entirely ignored, but which other biographers have considered very important, and which Charlotte herself confessed in the most heartrending way in her last novel, *Villette*—her feeling for one of her publishers, George Smith, who was much younger than herself. Charlotte saw him as a "true young English Gentleman." He seems to have been of good appearance, a bright, kind-hearted and gay young man who had shown an interest in Charlotte, who took it once more to be love. Now, however, she could not be deceived as easily as before. A strong faith was deeply rooted in her that if happiness existed in the world, it was not for her. And she did not dare to hope much—a fact which gave her greater perception. The bright young· man beside her was for her a symbol of happiness—and for a time she had timidly believed that perhaps she, too, might know this happiness, perhaps she, too, might become bright and healthy and happy, a hope expressed in her sudden interest in dress and in striking colours which she had never dared to wear before. But as she writes in *Villette*, "I learned in time that this benignity, this cordiality, belonged in no shape to me; it was a part of himself; it was the honey of his temper, it was the balm of his mellow mood; he imparted it, as the ripe fruit rewards·with sweetness the rifling bee; he diffused it about him, as sweet plants shed their perfume. Does the nectarine love either the bee or the bird it feeds? Is the sweet-briar enamoured of the air?" She knew it was empty, hollow, that it meant nothing to him. And for this reason she resigned it—she closed her eyes to the desired beauty for fear it might turn her into stone. But this curious "one-sided friendship," which was half-visionary, half-real, was not in vain. It formed the warmest and most moving part of *Villette*, Charlotte Brontë's masterpiece. In *Villette* George Smith appears as Dr. John, and I cannot agree with Lord David Cecil when he includes Dr. John among those characters of Charlotte Brontë's who are "mere tedious aggregations of good qualities, painted figure-heads of virtue like the heroes of Scott." Dr. John is the warmest creation of the unfulfilled desires of Charlotte Brontë's life, vibrating with feeling and having all that heartbreaking beauty of happiness which we have given up. "Good-night, Dr. John; you are good, you are beautiful, but you are not mine. Good-night, and God bless you!" Could any woman say this to a man who was not real enough to be embraced with love? And it is the intensity of his reality, explaining the despair of the frustrated heroine, that gives to the first part of the novel a poetic charm not unknown in the following lines of Cavafis:

> Like beautiful bodies dead that had not grown old
> And they shut them up, with tears in a splendid tomb adorning
> With roses at their heads and jasmine at their feet—
> Desires are like that, desires that have grown cold
> And not been satisfied; never vouchsafed one sweet
> Night time of pleasure or one gleam of morning.

There is an even closer parallel to these lines in *Villette*, a passage which is perhaps the most perfect Charlotte ever wrote.

Her lines, full of simple and restrained suffering without the usual defects of rhetoric and bad taste, so characteristic of her style, describe the strange burial of the letters of the beloved by the woman who has resigned her love. It is the description of the burial of the deepest desires in the life of a woman who wanted so much to live:

". . . A thought struck me—one of those queer fantastic thoughts that will sometimes strike solitary people. I put on my bonnet, cloak and furs, and went out into the city.

"Bending my steps to the old historical quarter of the town, whose hoar and overshadowed precincts I always sought by instinct in melancholy moods, I wandered on from street to street, till, having crossed a half-deserted 'place' or square, I found myself before a sort of broker's shop; an ancient place, full of ancient things.

"What I wanted was a metal box which might be soldered, or a thick glass jar or bottle, which might be stoppered or sealed hermetically. Amongst miscellaneous heaps, I found and purchased the latter article.

"I then made a little roll of my letters, wrapped them in oiled silk, bound them with twine, and, having put them in the bottle, got the old Jew broker to stopper, seal and make it airtight. While obeying my directions, he glanced at me now and then suspiciously from his frost-white eyelashes. I believe he thought there was some evil deed on hand. In all this I had a dreary something—not pleasure—but a sad, lonely satisfaction. The impulse under which I acted, the mood controlling me, were similar to the impulse and the mood which had induced me to visit the confessional. With quick walking I regained the pensionnat just at dark and in time for dinner.

"At seven o'clock the moon rose. At half-past seven, when the pupils and teachers were at study, and Madame Beck was with her mother and children in the salle-à-manger, when the half-boarders had all gone home, and Rosine had left the vestibule, and all was still—I shawled myself, and, taking the sealed jar, stole out through the first classe door, into the berceau and thence into the 'allée défendue.'

"Methuselah, the pear-tree, stood at the further end of this walk, near my seat: he rose up dim and grey, above the lower shrubs round him. Now Methuselah, though so very old, was of sound timber still; only there was a hole, or rather a deep hollow, near his root. I knew there was such a hollow, hidden partly by ivy and creepers growing thick round; and there I meditated hiding my treasure. But I was not only going to hide a treasure—I meant also to bury a grief. That grief over which I had lately been weeping, as I wrapped it in its winding sheet, must be interred.

"Well, I cleared away the ivy and found the hole; it was large enough to receive the jar and I thrust it deep in. In a tool-shed at the bottom of the garden lay the relics of building materials, left by masons lately employed to repair a part of the premises. I fetched thence a slate and some mortar, put the slate on the hollow, secured it with some cement, covered the whole with black mould, and finally, replaced the ivy. This done, I rested, leaning against the tree; lingering, like any other mourner, beside a newly-sodded grave."

AN INTRODUCTION TO MODERN GREEK POETRY

AN introduction to the poetry of a foreign country is one of the most difficult things to undertake. Poetry means language—the inmost essence of language—and since the days of Babel men have been condemned to speaking different languages. "Let us go down," God said, as we read in the Bible, "let us go down, and there confound the language of men that they may not understand one another's speech." This is true not only as regards countries, but also as regards individuals. In this article, however, I am not interested in the tragedy of individuals. I shall also say very little about the tragedy of the countries whose poetic voice is not understood by the world.

In spite of the curse of Babel I shall try to give you a picture of modern Greek poetry. In spite of all differences of language, all people have many things in common. There are things like life and death, love and hatred, nature and dreams which are common to all mankind.

All human beings come from the unknown to live in this world for a few years, trying to give a meaning to their lives, and then they go back to the unknown again. The questions of life, of the meaning of life and of death, are subjects we find in the poetry of all ages and all countries.

In order to give you a picture of modern Greek poetry, I shall try to show you what form these eternal questions take in the work of the national modern Greek poets. I shall speak to you about the question of life and death as we find it in the Greek ballads, and in the work of two nineteenth-century poets, who are considered the national poets of modern Greece, Solomos and Calvos.

The origin of the modern Greek ballads, just like the origin of the popular English ballads, cannot be easily traced. Various specialists think that most of the Greek ballads must be the work of eighteenth-century anonymous poets. What is certain is that some of these Greek ballads, like some of the English ballads, are among the most beautiful poems of their language. I shall first take a very short ballad—a very moving poem about nature and death, in which we see quite clearly what the world means to the anonymous Greek poets, or rather to the common Greek people. The metre of the modern Greek ballad is not very much unlike the usual metre of the English ballad and of the English church hymns. The Greek line is the "δεκαπεντασύλλαβος," one line of fifteen syllables. The stanza of the English ballad usually has two distichs of fourteen or fifteen syllables each, so that the stanza of an English ballad has more or less the same effect as two lines of a Greek ballad. The ballad is the one beginning καλότυχά 'ναι τά βουνά, and this is how I would translate it:

> You lucky mountains, lucky fields,
> You have no fear of Death;
> You don't expect the Murderer,
> But only lovely springs,
> Summers that make the mountains green,
> And strew the fields with flowers.

In modern Greek poetry, especially in the ballads, we find an astounding awareness of death. This awareness is not at all like the awareness of death we find in the English mediæval mystery plays and moralities, or in the Elizabethan plays.

O Death, thou comest when I had thee least in mind,

says "Everyman" in the well-known English mediæval morality. This line shows that death was not always in the people's mind, and that the writers of plays such as "Everyman" wrote them to remind people that they must be always prepared to leave the world. The Elizabethans, again, made so much fuss about death because death was a new discovery to them. A new age was then beginning for England, a new type of man, full of vitality and possibilities, was taking shape, and this new age and this new man, while they were becoming aware of their own potentialities, were also discovering their own limits—the worst of which is death. And that is why death plays such an important part in the great Elizabethan plays. In the modern Greek ballads, on the contrary, the people do not need to be reminded of death, as in "Everyman," and if they seem so aware of death, it is not because they have just discovered it. The Greeks have a very long history behind them, and this long history has given them the knowledge of human limits. The poets of the Greek ballads seem to be so aware of death because every Greek, even the least educated, has been given a profound wisdom by the history of his country. But this wisdom, this knowledge of human limits the modern Greek has, which makes his poetry so thoughtful and melancholy, does not make him accept these limits and resign himself to his fate. This same history the Greek has behind him and which gives him his wisdom, his irony and his scepticism, gives him also an astounding belief in some ideas, a strong sense of honour, and an unheard-of pride. The Greek of the ballads is melancholy because he knows that no one can escape death—but when death comes this same meditative person does not give up himself to the Murderer, to the φονιά, but, although he knows too well that he will be defeated, he wants to fight, and die an honourable death. The fight of the Greek "pallikari," the Greek hero with Death, is the subject of another Greek ballad, which I have translated as follows:

"Take off your clothes, young man, lay down
Your arms and cross your hands.
My name is Death and I have come
To take your soul away."
"I won't take off my clothes, I won't
Lay down my arms," he answered.
"You may be Death, but I won't let
You take my soul away.
We both are men, and both are brave,
Let us then go and fight,
Wrestle on iron threshing-floors,
Lest we destroy the country."
They went and fought like man with man
On iron threshing-floors.
Nine times the young man knocked down Death,
And Death was hurt at last.
He took the young man by his hair
And forced him to his knees.
"Death, leave my hair alone," he cried,
"And take me from the waist.
Then I shall show you what it is
To wrestle with a man."
But Death replied: "It is the hair
I like to grasp and hold;
The hair of boys and lively girls,
Of warlike men and children."

This poem is a wonderful illustration of the Greek's attitude to life. During this war the way in which the Greeks fought the invaders of their country made people wonder. What inner, spiritual power enabled the Greeks to fight as they fought? The poetry of the Greek ballads which throws light upon the psychology of the modern Greek gives also an explanation to this problem. And it is not only the poetry of the Greek ballads which shows what life and death and freedom mean to the Greek of today. It is the central theme of all modern Greek poetry.

Dionysios Solomos is considered the national poet of modern Greece. The words of the Greek national anthem are his; he lived during the war of Greek Independence and his poetry is burning with patriotism and the love of freedom; but, in spite of that, Solomos was not only a patriotic poet, and his poetry is significant not only for the Greeks. There is an excellent book about him in English by Romilly Jenkins, of Cambridge University, published three years ago. Solomos' poetry has a freshness— and at the same time a depth—which make him one of the most interesting poets of the nineteenth century. His poetry has such a freshness because when he started writing it was before the liberation of Greece, and the modern Greek language was something fresh, which had not been much used by deliberate poetry. Solomos could use in his poetry the simplest and most ordinary words such as "kalos" = good, "omorfos" = beautiful, "glykos" = sweet, words which the poets of a worn-out language rather avoid, and he could make poetry, a poetry full of freshness, out of them. There are some admirable lines, beginning

Ἔστησ' ὁ Ἔρωτας χορὸ
Μὲ τὸν ξανθὸν Ἀπρίλη. . .

which I have translated as follows:

Blond April dances with the God
Of Love, and Nature's happy.
And in the growing shade which hides
Riches of fragrant coolness,
One hears unheard-of, fainting songs
Of birds. Clear, lovely waters
Run into scented depths of earth,
And rob them of their perfumes,
And showing all the treasures of
Their sources to the sun,
They run hither and thither, mad,
And sing like nightingales.

AN INTRODUCTION TO MODERN GREEK POETRY 167

A butterfly which scented her
Sleep in the heart of lilies,
Played on the silent surface of
The lake with a small shadow.
—You who can see the spirits move,
What did you see to-night?
—The night was full of miracles,
The night was full of spells.

This lovely passage, full of the freshness of nature described
in a new, fresh language, is not only a charming description. It
is much more than that. This passage belongs to a long, un-
finished poem called "The Free Besieged," inspired by one of
the most stirring incidents of the Greek War of Independence,
the Siege of Missolonghi. Missolonghi, the Greek town where
Byron died, had been besieged by enemy forces so overwhelming
that there was no doubt about the issue of the struggle. In spite
of that the Greeks were not giving in. Mr. Jenkins in his book
on Solomos, says about the poem: "The scene is Missolonghi,
but Missolonghi now stands for the world of men. The pro-
tagonists are Greek heroes, but their adventures are those of the
human soul. We have passed from historical and political poetry
to Greek tragedy. The conflict of the rational soul in opposition
to the brute forces of matter, the weakness of the flesh, and the
temptations of the senses, are now the theme. The Besieged are
led into temptation, in order that they may overcome it and
win the crown that shall not be taken away from them. Brutality
and cruelty strive to intimidate them; their starving bodies are
tempted at the sight of the vigorous enemy, strong in the plenty
of unhampered supplies; the women must survive their children's slow death; the men must endure a final, heart-rending
failure of nerve on the part of the women, as the hour of dawn
draws nigh when the sortie is to be made; hopes of relief are
raised only to be dashed when it is seen that the approaching
squadron is not Greek. And last and most powerful of all, nature
and spring-time conspire to defeat their resolution by appearing
all round them in their most alluring manifestations. In vain:
they have the courage never to submit or yield—reason is triumphant, and the Besieged by their indomitable endurance become
finally and absolutely free."

This absolute freedom of man in life, a freedom which is there
as an attitude in spite of the facts of bondage, of failure and

death, pictured in a wonderful way by the Greek ballads in which man does not surrender to death, but wrestles with him on iron threshing-floors—this absolute freedom, which means everything to the Greek of today, is also the theme of our national poet's most important work, "The Free Besieged." An attitude of absolute freedom similar to the one we find in modern Greek literature we find in some works of Russian literature, in Dostoevsky's *Letters from the Underworld*, for instance. The hero of *Letters from the Underworld* speaks of the limitations of man, which make absolute freedom impossible. He describes them as a stone wall, and says: "Of course, I am not going to beat my head against a wall if I have not the necessary strength to do so; yet I am *not* going to *accept* that wall merely because I have run up against it, and have no means to knock it down." Yet, Dostoevsky's attitude of absolute freedom is expressed with too much passion while Solomos' attitude of absolute freedom has no bitterness in it—it is full of dignity and pride.

What could be more dignified than this verse from Εὐχαί, by Calvos, the other Greek national poet, in which he gave us a most moving self-portrait:

> No passion disturbs me—
> I strike the lyre
> And I stand upright
> By the open mouth
> Of my grave.

Calvos was born at the end of the eighteenth century in Zanthe, one of the loveliest Ionian Islands, restored to Greece and to freedom some years after his death by Great Britain. Although he was brought up in Italy, he left her for England, where as he says in one of his poems "the rays of sweet Freedom" nourished him. He lived in this country for many years and he died in this country. Married twice, both times to an English woman, he was deeply influenced by the manners, the thought and the poetry of this country. But in spite of that—or perhaps because of that—he is one of the two great national poets of Greece. When his native country—so weak against such a powerful enemy—rose, in 1821, in the desperate determination to die or to regain her freedom, he was so much stirred by the greatness of the event that he became a poet to proclaim its meaning

to the world. In his poetry we find the same attitude of absolute
freedom we found in the Greek ballads and in Solomos' poetry.
Here is a translation of one of his most important poems, his
"Ode to Death" (ὠδὴ πρὸς τὸν θάνατον), in which the poet suddenly finds himself in a very old temple:

Peaceful, frozen,
The vast wings
Of the deep night
Cover
The whole world.

Be silent here; there are bodies of Saints
Sleeping in this place.
Be silent here; do not disturb
The sacred rest
Of the dead.

I hear the fury
Of the raging wind;
It strikes violently; the windows
Of the temple open
Torn to pieces.

From the sky
Where the dark-winged
Clouds sail,
The moon throws
Its cold silver.

It lights up a cold,
White, silent piece of marble;
One sees on the grave
A censer without fire,
Candles without flame, and funeral cakes.

*   *   *

Look, the gravestone moves.
Look, from the cracks of the grave
A thin vapour comes out
And stands
In front of me.
It grows thicker; it takes
Human shape.
What are you? Tell me!
A creation, a phantom
Of my disturbed mind,
Or a human being
Living in graves?
Do you smile?

*   *   *

And the ghost speaks:

> —Don't ask me questions; don't search
> The inexpressible mystery
> Of death . . .
>
>   *   *   *

The ghost is the poet's mother:

> Oh, my son, my son,
> My dear child,
> Our fates are different
> And it is in vain that you try
> To embrace me.
> Do not cry. You had better smile.
>
>   *   *   *
>
> Why do you cry? You don't know
> What the fate of my soul is.
> And in this grave
> My body rests
> From pain.
>
> Oh, yes, life is an unbearable'
> Pain; the hopes,
> The tears, and the pleasures,
> The sweetness of the world
> Torture you.
> We the dead enjoy
> Eternal peace,
> Free from fear,
> Free from sorrow
> Our sleep is free from dreams.
>
> You, the cowards,
> When someone whispers
> The name of Death, tremble;
> But no one, no one
> Can escape Death.
>
> My son, you saw me breathing;
> The sun revolving
> Like a spider, folded me
> In light and in death
> Incessantly.
>
> The spirit which was my life
> Was a breath of God
> And went back to Him,
> My body was earth and it fell
> Here, in the grave.
> But the light of the moon
> Vanishes; I must leave you. . . .
>
>   *   *   *

Farewell, my son.
   —Oh, do not go!
Do not leave your son
In sorrow.

     But she has vanished.
And my eyes are open
In deep darkness.

—Now, now my lips
Could kiss
The knees of Death;

Where are the roses? Bring
Never-fading wreaths;
Give me the lyre; sing;
The terrible enemy
Became a friend.
How can Death, who kissed

The forehead of frail women,
Frighten
The heart of a man?

Who is in danger?
Now that I face
Death with courage
I hold the anchor
Of salvation.

The attitude of absolute freedom in facing Death with courage
is a theme we often find in modern Greek poetry. We found it
in the Greek ballad of the man wrestling with Death on iron
threshing-floors; we found it in Solomos' "Free Besieged"; we
found it in Calvos' "Ode to Death." If I had more space I could
give you many similar examples, from the work of our other important poets, Cavafis, Sikelianos, Kazantzakis, Seferis. I shall,
however, conclude with a poem by the young Greek poet Prevelakis, which was originally published in *Folios of New Writing*:

Death is frozen waiting outside my door.
Open to him! Open the door!
Because I still have a soul in my breast,
This morning, as I was passing by,
The cypresses presented arms
And the wet earth longed
For the handful of my dust.

Let us open and receive Death!
Because I still have a soul in my breast!
The standing furrows that I ploughed
This year also expect my sowing.

This poem, written just before this war, shows that the traditional theme of modern Greek poetry is still alive in the hearts of the young Greek poets.

MY FRIEND DEMETRIOS CAPETANAKIS

By Panayotis Canellopoulos

I speak of one who was my friend. It is by no means an easy and perfectly natural thing to be someone's friend. He knew it better than anyone. He had thought about friendship for a long time and with intense concentration. I came to know him when he was entirely occupied with thought. He was seventeen years old. I was his professor at the University of Athens. And I learnt a great deal from my pupil.

He died in London, at the Westminster Hospital, at the age of 32. He knew the hospital well. The year before, he had found himself there without knowing how or why. He did not wish to live. He had had enough, or rather he had much less than he needed; and it was precisely the clear knowledge of that fact which made him unwilling to live. It was in January, 1943. I was on a visit to London; and when he recovered consciousness—he had been unconscious for several hours—he asked to see me, and John Lehmann. I sat beside his bed, and he smiled. He decided to live again, for that one year. It was a concession to Death. For, in his view, it was life that expressed Death. His optimism was too great for him to be able to content himself with what others call life.

He was the most discreet and self-effacing of persons, in every sense. When he was present it was as if he was not there. And when he was not there you felt him quite close to you. He seemed something more than alive with his frail body, something more than robust with his delicate constitution, something more than dead in the sense that, even while still alive, he seemed already to have passed beyond his own life and death.

Athens, Heidelberg, Cambridge: those were the stages in his education after he had lived as a child in the atmosphere of seventeenth-century Paris. He knew, almost by heart, all Mme. de Sévigné's Letters. Later on, he rediscovered their author through reading Marcel Proust, seeing her in an entirely new light. Proust somewhere compares Mme. de Sévigné with Dostoevsky. An eccentric comparison? I do not think so; my friend united all three of them in a remarkable way in his own person —the Marquise, Dostoevsky and Proust.

His greatest adventure was Stefan George. I was a political prisoner, deported to a little Ægean island, when he came home from Heidelberg. He came to see me (he was very courageous and had a complete contempt for the police of the Metaxas régime). It was the only time we ever had a quarrel—a quarrel without words. I was severe with him, and he had become cruel —cruel towards himself. He was trying to escape the judgment of his own conscience. Stefan George had imposed on him for some years the laws of his own world. They were laws without any meaning. My friend realized later that the new state founded by Stefan George had no place for citizens, and as for the laws they had no existence either; there was only the icy figure of the law-giver and nothing else. The experience was so shattering for my friend that he very nearly failed to recover from it. And it was no great prophet that saved him. Stefan George was conquered by *Robinson Crusoe* and the poetry, or rather the life so miraculously without significance, of Thomas Gray. Scarcely had he arrived in Cambridge when he sent me two letters, in which he told me of these discoveries. In another letter he talked of John Donne and William Blake. He was cured. And later on he wrote his English article on Stefan George, a painful and ironic epilogue to the whole affair.

At the time when he left Greece to go to Cambridge, in 1939, he had been studying English for only a few months. When I escaped from occupied Greece, in 1942, I found him transformed into an English poet. English had become his own tongue. It was as if the English language had chosen *him*—as if she had need of him.

It was always the same with him: he completed his experience of a thing in the first moment of awareness; and so it was that the thing itself—pleasure, achievement, pain—always became wearisome to him. He not only anticipated the corn in the moment of sowing, but even the sowing itself as the sower lifted his arm.

He published two essays on Rimbaud, one in Greek, the other in English; the first before his adventure with Stefan George, the other after. He had himself lived in the "drunken boat"; it was for him, far more than for Rimbaud, the Ark of the Flood turned into a bobbing cork: a cosmic disenchantment. Later on, in one of his English poems, he imagines himself as Abel, sitting beside his brother Cain, "in cinemas half-lit By scenes of peace that always turned to slaughter." But he survived his cosmic disenchantment, not as Rimbaud did—Rimbaud, who after having seen "la blanche Ophélia flotter comme un grand lys," became a dealer in exotic merchandise—but by continuing, in spite of all that he knew and suffered, to want to be loved. Yes, to *be* loved. He could not stand Rainer Maria Rilke, because that poet of God, of women, and of the music of intangible beings, had said that, in love, everything lies in the act of loving.

There is something majestic in this controversy. The problem goes right back to the conception of the creation of the world, to the very moment before the birth of light.

Incidentally, my friend knew very well that clear vision has little to do with light. It is not in light, it is rather in darkness, that lucidity is born. That was what my friend believed; and when I was in London, in January, 1943, to confirm him in the view which he already held, I wrote a sonnet in Greek in which I said that "love and hate are both shadows." When he heard those lines, he triumphed. He triumphed, but I could not help feeling sad myself.

When my friend triumphed—and that was why I had the right to feel sad about him—it was always an act of resistance; never an offensive, never an attack with the intention of conquering. Conquering what? he would have asked. The truth of suffering? But suffering is a reality; it has no need to be a truth. It is what does not exist that seeks to become true. My friend did not want to enter the territory of things that do not exist—joy, happiness. Nevertheless, a smile of joy would often cross his face. But that was different; it was the smile of a child's contentment. Though he knew beforehand what every kind of experience was like, he had in a way never left the world of childhood.

My friend's smile: one can only say that it was an archaic smile. Egyptian Pharaohs, Greek archaic statues, Etruscan gods— do not all those strange countenances seem to belong at the same time to childhood and an impossible kind of maturity? It was almost the same feeling that my friend's face gave me. Often, while looking at it, I felt that I was like someone who has to unravel an impossible problem. And the impossible is life itself. I would look at my friend's face, and an ever graver conviction would come to me: that death itself is what is impossible.

PART III

THE BREEZES OF FREEDOM

(Translated from the Greek of Pantelis Prevelakis)

THE breezes of freedom blow all round me!
My body, like the standing harp left
idle in the midst of the moaning orchestra,
trembles quietly,
forgotten by the pains, by suffering,
forgotten by necessity.
I listen to the quiet resound:
resonator of the universe,
secret, imperceptible response,
—o miracle of love!—
top of a high tree
moved by the songs of the birds.

THE SUNSET

(*Translated from the Greek of Pantelis Prevelakis*)

THE sunset entered the room,
a red lion.
His reflection fell on the mirror
and I felt his tender paw
touching my bare feet.
I stooped under my table,
that was sanctified by the work of the day,
and I saw him, the sun, kissing my feet
with his red tongue.

ANNIVERSARY

(Translated from the Greek of Odysseus Elytis)

I BROUGHT my life as far as this
Point that struggles
Always by the sea
Youth on the rocks, hand
To hand with the wind
Where is a man going
Who is nothing but a man
Measuring his green moments with
Their coolness, the visions of his
Ears with waters, his remorse with wings
O Life
Of the boy that becomes a man
Always by the sea when the sun
Teaches him to breathe forward where the shadow
Of a seagull vanishes

I brought my life as far as this
White addition black total
A few trees and a few
Wet pebbles
Light fingers to caress a forehead
What forehead
The expectations wept all night and no one is any more
No one is
To make us hear a free step
To make us see the sunrise of an untired voice
To make the ships bounding by the jetty write
A name of a purer azure in their horizon
A few years, a few waves
Sensitive rowing
In the harbours round the love

I brought my life as far as this
Bitter cutting in the sand that will vanish
—whoever saw two eyes touching his silence

And mingled their suns enclosing thousands of worlds
Must remind the other suns of his blood
Nearer the light
There is a smile that repays the flame—
But here in the unaware landscape vanishing
In an open and merciless sea,
Success is dispersed
Whirling feathers
And moments that were bound to the earth
Hard earth under the impatient
Soles, earth made for giddiness
Dead volcano.

I brought my life as far as this.
A stone promised to the liquid element
Beyond the islands
Below the waves
Near the anchors
—When keels pass vehemently rending
A new obstacle they overcome
And with all its dolphins hope shines
Gain of the sun in a human heart—
The nets of doubt draw out
A salt figure
Hewn with pains
Indifferent white
Turning the void of its eyes towards the sea
Supporting the infinite.

A RECOLLECTION

By William Plomer

It had been clear for many months that an insidious illness was gaining upon him, and before the end of 1943, when he was afflicted with a slow wasting fever, I think Demetrios understood clearly that it was mortal; but in that loneliness of the condemned man or woman his perceptions seemed to grow keener than ever, ideas crowded in upon him as if to say good-bye, and the characters of his friends showed themselves in high relief against the turmoil of the world.

One evening, about the end of October, there was an exceptionally thick fog, and I decided to pilot him as best I could to his door in Prince of Wales's Terrace before making my own way home. It was a case of the blind leading the blind, and even if we had had a torch we should have gained little. On certain nervous systems a thick London fog acts like a kind of drug: the absence of perspective, the enfeebled sense of locality and direction, the familiar suddenly turning into the unknown, the muffled or suddenly magnified sounds and lights, occasional voices clearly defined in the absence of traffic—these things help to produce an effect of excited hallucination. I told Demetrios how in a similar fog a bird had suddenly perched on the handlebar of a bicycle which someone was pushing slowly and had remained there. Characteristically and rather intensely, he said, "How strange!"

That exclamation, and "How wonderful!" were frequent utterances of his. They used sometimes to remind me of Pater's saying that "it is the addition of strangeness to beauty, that constitutes the romantic character in art," and that the addition of curiosity to the desire of beauty constitutes the romantic temper. Demetrios certainly had the romantic temper: he had the curiosity that discovers the extraordinary even in the apparently commonplace. As for a London fog, it had for him, he said, associations with Dickens, whom he had read when a boy in the dry glare of Attica. We of the north and the west turn towards the sun; we look to the south and the east and the past for beauty and strangeness; we have looked with curiosity and passion to the Mediterranean, our Goethes and Byrons to Italy and Greece, our

Flauberts to Carthage, our Gissings to Rome; we have looked to the Arab countries and towards Asia for the unknown and the exotic, the strangely stirring. But Demetrios was a son of a country where it is common to talk of Europe as of something distant and apart and of America as a vast and remote land of promise: in the lucid aridity of Greece he had dreamt of the north and the west and the present, the blond energies of the German, the Englishman dreaming and smiling in his fogs, the fantastic activity of the American.

With his romantic temper he was particularly drawn to melancholy and passion, especially the incandescent passion that may burn like a jet in a circumscribed environment or a frustrated heart, or that bursts out in desperate acts, or in the creation of enormous myths, or in confession transmuted into art. Hence his interest in Dostoevsky, Rimbaud, Stefan George or Emily Dickinson, the fascination exerted upon him by the Brontës, his quick response to a mention of a picture by Géricault or a poem by Christina Rossetti, his knowledge of Proust and Balzac, his pleasure at being given the plays of Balzac—which he did not know—because of the one about Vautrin, his eagerness to know every detail of some private or public tale of a contemporary *crime passionel*. The interest in passion implies a love of excitement. I have seen him tease a black cat in a garden on a summer night, not to hurt or annoy it, but to excite it: the cat, I think, recognized in him a congenial nature. He was excited by crowded underground trains on winter's nights in the black-out. He was excited, as a novelist might be, by manifestations of feminine jealousy, unusual ambitions, renunciations, hopeless love affairs, unpredictable impulses. He was excited not only by films, but by the fact that they were visible in dark and crowded theatres.

His interest in the American character was unmeasured. He was very well read in American fiction: that, and the films, seemed chiefly to have formed his vision—no ordinary vision—of American life, for he had never been in the United States. The arrival in London of so many Americans was highly interesting to him, and although he made among them at least one valued acquaintance, I think he was a little disillusioned by the cumulative effect of a number of trivial chance contacts: the "strangeness" was not dispersed, but was perhaps not quite what he had expected; and when he read a novel called *Studs Lonigan* he was suddenly overcome with revulsion at the vision of a kind of uncouthness that was like poison to him. I think if he had been able to visit America, the impact of that country upon him might have produced a vivid and original interpretation, still largely if not entirely sympathetic. In England he had lived long enough to discover that we are more various and have more warmth than is at first apparent; he had also discovered in us (so he wrote) a balance of gentleness and stubbornness, which I think he was coming to value more and more; and he had fallen in love with our language, "the poetic language *par excellence,*" and could already use it with power and originality. It is no good lamenting what he might have written, but it is good to examine and ponder over what he did write, particularly in verse. In literary as in personal relationships, if an Englishman has something to give a Greek, a Greek may enchant an Englishman by such gifts as those of spontaneity, intensity, and demonstrativeness.

Of his physical presence the chief feature was his dark eyes, glowing with intelligence and feeling. He was slight in build and had delicate, nervous hands of an almost Asiatic fineness. His nose might have seemed a little too large if he had not had such a placid-looking mouth, such a fine smooth forehead and clear skin, so that somehow the whole face was harmonious: though not conventionally beautiful it had a kind of radiance, an effect of luminosity which indeed gained him an affectionate nickname. Its harmony was no doubt derived from the balance of a shapely character with an understanding that was speculative and not aggressive.

There was a dreadful irony about his lying in a hospital bed endowed in memory of Neville Chamberlain and "his great efforts for peace." In it he lay with the calmness that comes from intellectual and emotional strength. I had found that, at least in private life, Demetrios showed, unlike many Greeks, little interest in politics. His feelings about the war and his country were probably too deep to be expressed. His mind ranged mostly in the untrammelled world of the imagination. He had achieved more and had endeared himself more than he perhaps knew, though I believe he suspected, and I hope the suspicion was strong enough to be of some comfort to him.